BeThat
Kinky Girl

*10% of all proceeds from the sale of this book
are donated to charities dedicated to supporting
girls and women around the world.*

BeThat
Kinky Girl

Ignite Your Passions and Be Seductive

TINA O'CONNOR

Be That
BOOKS®
PUBLISHING

Be Inspired.
Be Motivated.
Be Entertained.

Library and Archives Canada Cataloguing in Publication

O'Connor, Tina, author Be that kinky girl / Tina O'Connor.

(Be that ; 3) Issued in print and electronic formats. ISBN 978-0-9879154-3-6 (pbk.).--ISBN 978-0-9879154-9-8 (html).-- ISBN 978-1-927897-00-3 (html)

1. Women--Sexual behavior. 2. Sexual excitement. 3. Sex instruction. I. Title.

HQ29.O26 2014   306.7082   C2014-906631-7   C2014-906632-5

Cover photo and author photo by TLM Productions (Wendell Tenove)

Interior photos:

TLM Productions (Wendell Tenove);

14, 18, 24, 64, 82, 104, 111, 114, 134, 140, 144

Tina O'Connor; 107, 124, 154

Shutterstock; 3, 15, 40 50, 54, 84, 86

Cover and text design by Tania Craan

Published in Canada by Be That Books® Publishing Inc.

SBN-10: 1-927897-04-1

ISBN-13: 978-1-927897-04-1

Printed and bound in Canada

This book is dedicated to my husband, Ryan.
Your unwavering support, love and friendship makes
me the luckiest kinky girl in the universe.

CONTENTS

Sexologist and Mom

There is nothing more powerful than a woman who has made up her mind. This is especially true when it comes to sex. A ton of thoughts about sex swirl around a woman's head while she's dating, getting more serious, deciding to settle down and then, finally, having children. How she perceives sex in each moment will make or break her sex life.

As a sexologist and mother, I've come to the conclusion that a big reason why sex can become increasingly difficult, sporadic and unfulfilling once we have kids is...(drum roll please)...we need to constantly recreate a new sexual rhythm with our partner. For example, we have a baby and discover that sex during naps is perfect, but then the baby stops napping. When the kids are older, we discover there is a two-hour window while they are watching their favorite movie, but then they start being aware of "Mommy and Daddy time." Once they become teenagers, our kids know exactly what we're up to, and it can sexually paralyze even the most connected couple.

As well, there seems to be a lot of couple anger where kids are involved — fighting about who's going to do what with the kids, who's going to clean up, who's responsible for cooking. Very few women are willing to have sex with someone she is angry with.

Instead of sex being a constant, wonderful experience that keeps us connected to our partner, sex becomes complicated. A constantly changing entity that needs to be renegotiated. Which is, quite frankly, just another chore on a long list. And we all know talking about our sexual needs, wants and desires is one of the most difficult conversations we can have. It's much easier to avoid and not make the time.

Hold on. Let's stop right there and reassess.

Sex is important. And it is something we need to fight for in our relationship. Why? There are so many valid reasons. Just one: being able to connect with another human being at such an intimate level is a gift too many don't get to experience. Luckily, having a good sex life doesn't have to be difficult or complicated.

You simply need to make up your mind that a good sex life is what you want.

Which is why you need to read Tina O'Connor's book, *Be That Kinky Girl*, a book chock-full of tips to not only spice things up in the bedroom and embrace your inner kinky girl, but also to really connect with your partner and build a deeper intimacy.

The book you are about to read will give you a thrilling guide to stepping out of your comfort zone and getting your partner to go along for the ride. I wish you the best of luck in your endeavors and believe you are in the best of hands with Tina as your guide.

— Dr. Trina E. Read,
sexologist, mom and bestselling author of
Till Sex Do Us Part: Make Your Married Sex Irresistible

Well, here I am once again, sitting in the privacy of Starbucks to write my third book, Be That Kinky Girl. If you've read either of my other books, Be That Girl or Be That Mom, you will know that I only write books when I am inspired to create change in my own life, and I only write what I want to write when I want to write it! So, why Be That Kinky Girl? As I write this, I have been married for 14 years and have been with the same wonderful man for 23 years. Yes, we were young when we met ... really young, but there was a passion and a connection between us that could not be ignored! We have always had an incredible sex life.

WHAT??!! OK, I will not lie to you. We are normal people, and we have experienced ups and downs throughout the years, even when it comes to the old in-out game. I know that I lied to myself during the lows, reassuring myself that it was OK not to have sex with my husband for extended periods of time. I told myself that we still had all the steam and that nothing was wrong. In reality, I was missing the intimacy, and so was my husband. The downs never lasted long, because both of us were committed to communicating and making our marriage not just work, but bubble with passion and joy.

That was not always easy. Looking back, it is so clear to me what the issue was. I could blame it all on having three children, but to be frank, we had low points even before we started having children. The lows coincided directly with my frame of mind or my husband's. But I will be honest: The times that my husband has turned down my proposition for a little nookie have been few and far between. If it happened more frequently, I would certainly have been worried. Yet I found it easy to reject his advances when I was not in the mood, without much regard for how he might feel. During my low times, I didn't think about sex, and I certainly wasn't missing it. At least that's what I told myself. *I don't need it!*

Now that I am older, I am also wiser to the ways of lovemaking: They don't call them the dirty thirties for nothing! I know that I deserve to have intimacy in my life, with myself and with others. It is okay to be sexual and to find intense pleasure in the stimulation, meditation and release that sex can bring. I do not believe that my age alone has released some of my inhibitions — rather, it is my mindset.

Why "kinky"?

According to the Merriam-Webster Dictionary, *kinky* is defined as *involving or liking unusual sexual behavior.*

In my opinion, the key word in this definition is "unusual," that which is not normally or usually done.

If you keep doing the same things, you will continue to get the same results. If you picked up this book, you are ready to take your sex life to the next level, whatever that is for you.

What is your definition of kinky? To my way of thinking, kinky refers to anything that is not strictly the missionary position! No matter what you like in the bedroom, it's OK! Every woman is going to have her own level of "kink." For you, it may start out with new positions, new locations or new attire. For others, kinky might involve handcuffs or blindfolds or couples' clubs. Whatever it is for you, embrace it and get excited about trying new things! Whether you have explored your deepest desires but aren't sure how to get it or you feel like you and your partner have gotten complacent in your lovemaking, I want to help you realize all your dirty little desires and help you have a more fulfilling, passionate, incredible, delicious, rewarding, relaxing, stimulating and exciting sex life! You are worth it. Intimacy and sex are good for us in many ways.

I aim to inspire more happiness and joy in women all over the world through the bliss of sex. So get ready to get kinky — it's about to get steamy in here!

CHAPTER 1

First, Free Your Mind

• • • • • • • • • • • • • •

"A great figure or physique is nice, but it's self-confidence that makes someone really sexy."
– Vivica A. Fox

Having sex — and receiving pleasure from sex — is a form of meditation and is a way to free your mind and your soul from the rush and buzz of everyday things. If you're doing it right, you will be totally immersed in the experience ... enjoying the pleasure you receive, as well as enjoying any pleasure you give out.

EXERCISE

Next time you have sex with a partner, try only thinking about how good everything feels. Tell yourself that it feels awesome, and that it's OK to feel that good! Clear your mind of any other thought and really allow yourself to be in the moment with your partner. Think of each touch, each lick, each stroke. Close your eyes and focus only on the pleasure of the moment. If any other thoughts come into your head, release them without judgment and get back to the nitty-gritty ... *he just did what to you??!!* Lucky girl.

It Starts with YOU. Confidence is Key.

In order to feel comfortable about yourself and others in a sexual way, you must have confidence and love for yourself and your body. This is essential for creating more passion in your life. Every person is different. Each body is different. You must learn to love your body as it is right now. You must treat your body with kindness and love. We all have insecurities about our bodies, and we also have things we love about our bodies. If you want to be more kinky, you need to go back to the beginning and create a better vision of you. You feel a certain way about your body because of your thoughts. Once you are aware of that, you will give yourself the power to change!

Remember back to the days of being a child, when you discovered your "hot buttons" for the first time, usually by accident. Once you discovered them, did you keep pushing them? Have you always enjoyed touching your body? Did you, at one time, enjoy touching your body but have since let go of that? Have you just started WANTING to touch your body? I want to help you discover some ways to love yourself and your body. I want you to WANT to touch yourself with love and pleasure. It feels good for a reason. Yes, from a purely anthropological standpoint, we desire sexual contact to ensure that procreation happens and that our genes continue on. From a universal standpoint, we are just meant to feel good. When we feel good, more good comes. Our sole purpose is to feel good. Imagine if everyone in the world felt good? Wouldn't that be nice?

Let's focus on getting YOU feeling great, for now. With small bites, together, we can eat the world!

From this day forward, you are a goddess. You are a sexy, beautiful, passionate woman with a lust for life and a gorgeous body that will inspire desire in others. You might be curvy, you might be thin, you might be tall, or short, you might be pregnant ... with twins ... no matter what skin you're in, sexiness comes from your thoughts, and it is transmitted into action by your body. You will become the woman that you think you are, so it's time to start considering the ways you talk to yourself about your body.

Mirror Challenge, Part 1

Do this every day for 21 days. In the comfort and privacy of your bathroom, strip down to your skin. Set a timer for five minutes. Stare at yourself in the mirror for the full five minutes. A full-length mirror works best for this task, as you want to be able to see your whole body. Take notice of your thoughts as you are looking at your body. Look into your own eyes and smile. Look at your arms, your shoulders, your neck, your chest and your breasts. Turn around and look at your ass in the mirror. Look at your pussy, if you can! (This is tricky and may require a handheld mirror.) How do you feel about your body? Do you instantly cringe at the way your breasts look (too big, too small, too saggy)? Do you loathe your muffin top, hate the way your belly button sinks in or pokes out? How about the cellulite on your legs? Time to do a little "airbrushing" in your mind ... because you are JUST RIGHT the way you are right now!

On Day 1, analyze your thoughts about your body. This will be the only day that you are allowed to assess your current thoughts about your body. On Day 2 and forward, you must try not to judge your body. Just stare at yourself and be aware of your body, as it is right now. Just look and don't think! Look at the shape of your body, the shape and size of your breasts, the size and color of your nipples, the curves of your hips and your ass, the shape of your arms and legs, and do not judge them. This is not easy to

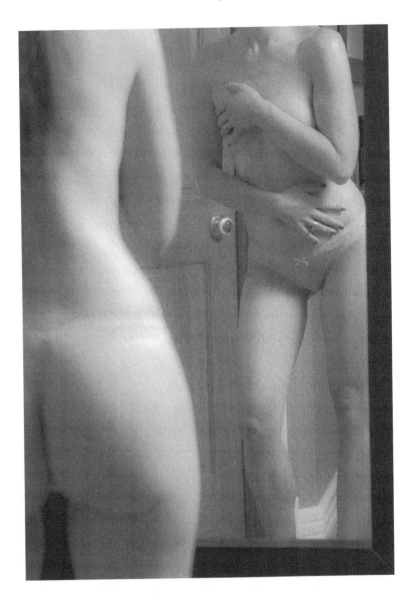

do, especially if you've been practicing negative self-talk regarding your body for a long time. It's important to note that this is a process. Be gentle with yourself, and each day that you look in the mirror, try to see the beauty that stands before you. It's important that you stop nitpicking every little piece of your body and love your whole body as it is, right now. So, how do you do that? It all starts with you being able to look at yourself and acknowledge yourself and your body for what they are right now, perfect for you in every way.

Each time you strip down and look at yourself in the mirror, assess how you feel. When you have a negative thought about a part of your body, don't let it get you down! Instead, immediately switch your focus to a part of your body that you do like. Insert positive thoughts whenever you can. Send every part of your body your love. Love your smile. Love your breasts, your ass, your pussy. Love yourself enough to feel good about every part of your body. If you find yourself thinking things like, "I hate the way my breasts look ... my nipples just sag after all that breast-feeding ... and they are soft and not perky anymore," you need to change that! While you may not love all of your parts (yet), there are surely parts you do like or things about your least favorite parts that are actually benefits to you. If you've been talking down to yourself about your breasts, here are some examples of positive things you can say to yourself to help change your thinking about them. Some breast examples:

"My breasts might be saggy, but they are so sensitive!"

"I have incredible cleavage with these beauties."

"I can wear any shirt I want with these little beauties and I don't really need a bra, except if I want to add a size or two!"

"I love that I can store things in my cleavage ... who needs a purse!?"

"Hitting my partner in the face with my beautiful breasts adds an element of excitement and danger to our sex life!"

If you dislike your belly but love your legs, when you strip down in the mirror, focus on your legs and how much you like them. Don't pay a lot of attention to your belly (or other parts that currently bother you). When you focus negative energy on anything, it is still energy, and it won't make you feel good about you. So focus on the good! Focus on what you do enjoy about your body and how your body is a source of pleasure and joy for you and others.

It is really incredible what changes when you are comfortable in your skin and when you appreciate the body you have been given. The more you love yourself, the better you will treat yourself. When you treat yourself better, you will begin to see transformations happening in your life. You are given only one body and you can literally "think" your way to a better you! Being happy with yourself as you are now can have an amazing impact on you. While you may love yourself, there may be things about your body that you would like to change. Fortunately, there are some things you will be able to change (weight). Unfortunately, there will always be things that you can never change (your feet). Loving yourself as you are allows you to be happy right now, and it also allows you to love the parts of you that you can never change. When you love and respect yourself and treat yourself well, you will be able to more easily change the things about your body that you do have control over. "Thinking" your way to a better body is possible. As I always say, you've got to fake it till you make it and just Be That Girl!

What would your ideal body be? If you could wave a magic wand and change anything, what would it be? Let's pretend that you have the ability to "airbrush" yourself right now. Part of being able to change things about your body that are modifiable is seeing yourself as already having your ideal body. There is no magic wand, but if you can see yourself as your ideal in your mind, you can make magic happen! See yourself having the attributes you desire when you look in the mirror. The more clearly you can do this, the more positivity you will create around your body and the more the Universe will respond by sending you positive energy. This exercise will change the way you feel about yourself RIGHT NOW, without changing a single physical thing. This is the goal. The way you feel about YOU will help you decide whether you want to change things about yourself (weight, breast size, cellulite) in the future. For now, just be happy with what you have.

"You get what you get, and you don't get upset."

When you pass your desires and wishes onto the Universe and you are happy NOW, you will find that everything you desire comes.

The better you feel about yourself, the better you will treat yourself. This will generally result in a better physical image over time, because you will treat your body better (now that you know you deserve it), and more happiness. No one can make you happy, not even your own body. That is strictly your mind's job. Happiness is a choice, a state of mind. Will you choose to be happy with you, starting today? You are definitely worth it!

I used to have incredibly negative self-talk when it came to my body. It's hard to ignore the external imagery and opinions of others in our lives. It's either not enough or too much ... does "just right" exist? Of course it does. You are already "just right," right now. Once you believe it, you will set yourself free.

Changing your thinking takes time, diligence, consistency and commitment. And you are worth it.

Mirror Challenge, Part 2

When your 21-day exercise with the mirror ends, you will start Part 2 of this exercise. Each day for 21 more days, return to the comfort of your bathroom or bedroom mirror. Set your timer for five minutes. This time, be sure to strip down in front of the mirror and watch yourself removing your clothes. As you are removing your clothing, think about how amazing you and your body are. Once you are naked, look in the mirror and smile. Now, touch yourself somewhere ... anywhere. Just in one place, any place you feel inspired by that day. Try to switch it up a bit and explore the feeling of other parts of your body each time. You will learn which spots need you!

Here are a few examples of some touches to try:

- Rub your arms, shoulders and neck with cream and watch yourself doing it.
- Rub your feet with cream.
- Slap your own ass. Try having your back to the mirror and crank your head around so you can see yourself in the mirror. Put on a kinky smile. Simple as that.
- Grab your breasts with both hands and squish them together into a bundle of joy. Lean over and look at your cleavage in the mirror. Tweak your nipple(s) if you feel so inclined.
- Wet your fingers with spit and rub them slowly on your nipples.
- Find your clitoris and touch it. I hope you know where it is! A little wetness will go a long way in this area.

Remember, this is only a five-minute exercise! If you've never felt comfortable touching yourself, first, let me reassure you that it is OK to touch yourself. No one needs to know. We are all at different stages when it comes to our sexuality. Slapping your ass may be way out of your comfort level at this stage of the game, while others of you may be bringing your toys into the bathroom for the five minutes of pleasure that I am blessing you with every day. It's OK. Getting more kinky means pushing yourself outside of your comfort level, just a little — or a lot, if you're up for it. I want you to grow. I want you to be kinky. I want you to be satisfied. I want you to be happy. Do what you're comfortable with and then let me push you a little further.

Please note: Your body is yours, and it is your responsibility to decide who can tell you what to do with it. You may have religious, parental, cultural or other societal beliefs that frown upon sex for pleasure and even on pleasuring yourself. I will not tell you to do anything you are not prepared to do! But I implore you to expand your own thinking about the Universe and what the energy of the world wants for you. Joy, happiness, pleasure and desire should all be positive emotions. Use them!

If you have a chance, go nude around other people where it is appropriate. On a nude or topless beach, let it all out. If you are at a women-only club where clothing is optional, try wearing your birthday suit. There is a fabulous spa with a water circuit in Toronto where you are free to be nude around lots of other women. I found it interesting to watch as small groups of girls would come into the water circuit pools. All of them would start off wearing their bathing suits. Within 20 minutes, one of the girls would take her top off ... seeing that everyone else was doing it. Then the others would follow. It's all about comfort and ease with your body, and only your opinion matters when it comes to your body. If you approve of your body, your confidence will shine to others all around you. Your beauty will radiate, and that's what people will notice about you. Your nipples should be allowed to catch the direct waves of the sun as you lay on your beach chair, once in a while! Your body should be treated with respect, kindness, love and tenderness. It should be set free sometimes! The more comfortable you are with how perfect your body is, just the way it is, the more you will love and want to share your body with others.

Once you're comfortable with yourself, it's time to explore what you like and need in the bedroom...

CHAPTER 2

What Do YOU Like in the Bedroom?

. . . .

*"'Sexy' is being independent,
being confident and having fun."*
– Mollie King

I hope you are enjoying practicing the mirror exercise. Successfully continuing it will increase your self-esteem and your self-confidence about your body. The touch part of the mirror exercise is very useful in helping you identify what you like to have done and to which areas of your body.

Think about your sexual history. If you haven't had one yet, don't worry — we'll get you there soon enough! Think about how sex has been for you in the past. Do you enjoy it? Do you loathe the thought of it? Does your partner know what to do to give you pleasure? Do you just try to get it over with? Do you always have to pleasure yourself after he is done, because you didn't get what you needed?

It's time to take responsibility for your sexual success! Only you know what you want, and only you can ensure you get it.

So, what do you like?

It may be easier for you to think about what you don't like as a way of determining what you do like!

EXERCISE

It's time to make a little "pleasure" wish list. You have just won the pleasure lottery, and whatever you ask for will be given to you. What's it going to be? Write down a list of five (or more) things you enjoy when it comes to being intimate with your body. You may enjoy some things sometimes and different things at other times. Try to really delve into what it is that gets you wet and makes you scream for more!

Here are some examples:

1. I love it when my partner kisses me passionately and lovingly, for a long time. I love feeling his arms wrapping me up into a bundle or lovingly grasping my hair, while he kisses me with desire. The longer, the better.

2. I love having my clothes ripped off with intensity. I want my partner to let me know that he needs me now!

3. I love having my breasts [touched, fondled, licked, sucked, tweaked, slapped, squeezed, gently rubbed with moisture, pulled, pinched, kissed]. Pick your pleasure.

4. I love it when my partner rubs the tip of his cock all over my pussy, without inserting it. The way he strokes my clit with his tip makes me squirm with intense desire!

5. I love touching myself, and I know just how to do it. Not too hard, not too soft, and I know just when to go faster or slower. I am always able to pleasure myself with love, and my "special toys" are always a good addition.

6. I love a nice, long massage of my entire body from my partner.

He teases me by occasionally lightly touching my panties or softly breezing past my breast, and it really gets me in the mood!

7. I love sensuously pleasuring my partner with my hand and my mouth. I love the way his cock feels in my moist hand, and I love the way it tastes. Turning him on is a big turn-on for me.

What "does it" for you? You really may not know what it is that you like because you haven't explored it enough or because you just haven't given it much thought. If you had a difficult time with the exercise above, it may just be that you don't know how to *express* what you like. It's likely that you haven't written down your sexual needs before, so be easy on yourself. Next time you have a sexual encounter, be conscious of what you enjoy and what you don't. Knowing what you don't like is very important, and you should never continue doing anything that doesn't feel good, even if your partner really enjoys it. Come back to this exercise after you've had some time to think about it, if you need to, but make sure you do it.

The biggest piece of having a healthy, robust, exciting sexual life is for you to know what makes you tick and what's going to make you tock!

The best way to explore your body is on your own. Whenever I write about or think about masturbating, I think of the song "I Touch Myself" by the Divinyls. The lyrics are awesome!

"I love myself

I want you to love me

When I'm feelin' down

I want you above me

I search myself

I want you to find me

I forget myself

I want you to remind me

I don't want anybody else

When I think about you

I touch myself"

This song really exemplifies my thoughts on exciting, kinky sex. You have to love yourself, and you have to touch yourself! You have to want someone else. You have to know what you want and then have someone else discover you and provide you what you desire. Once they know your body and you, they will be able to bring you pleasure when you have forgotten that you need it.

So, it's time to touch yourself!

What is masturbation? Defined by the Merriam-Webster Dictionary, masturbation is "erotic stimulation especially of one's own genital organs commonly resulting in orgasm and achieved by manual or other bodily contact exclusive of sexual intercourse, by instrumental manipulation, occasionally by sexual fantasies, or by various combinations of these agencies."

EXERCISE

While you may judge your own body, you may find it easier to be honest with yourself than with a partner! Once per week (or more if you are so inclined!), I want you to pay special attention to yourself for at least half an hour. If you've never "touched yourself" before or you just forget how, don't worry — we'll take it nice and slow for now. If you are skilled in this department, I still want you to embark on this exercise, and I want to encourage you to take your self-love to a deeper level.

Find a quiet, private area of your home where you feel comfortable. Often, you will choose your bedroom, and I think this is a fitting place, but everyone's location will be personal. Be sure that your half-hour will not be interrupted ... you have important work to do, girl! Now it is time to seduce yourself, just as you would expect someone else to do! Here are some ideas to get you in the mood for a little alone time:

Run a spa-like bath

Make it nice and hot. Bring in a glass of wine, tea or a refreshing chilled beverage of your choosing. Indulge yourself with a light snack … chocolate or cheese or fruit. Immerse yourself in the bath, close your eyes and just relax for two to five minutes. Slow your breathing down by consciously taking longer, deeper breaths. Send love to your body.

Wash your body with a bar of soap. Lovingly wash your feet, your legs and your armpits and use care when you touch yourself. As you wash your body, pay extra attention to your pleasing areas … rub your nipples with the bar and keep washing as much as you want! Use the bar to cleanse your pussy. Rub the bar slowly back and forth on your clit … adjust the pressure to suit the intensity of your mood. Increase or decrease the pressure as you desire. Wash your ass and see what kind of pleasure, if any, you get from rubbing the bar over your anus. When you are soapy enough, put the bar down.

Now, using your hands, feel your body. Rub your hands all over your soapy body; rub your legs, your feet, your arms and your back. The soap will make it easy for your hands to glide smoothly and easily over your delicious body, and it will intensify the feeling of your own touch. Use your hands to touch your pleasure areas. Increase the pressure and intensity of your touch in the areas that feel they need it. You have two hands, so don't be shy! Use one for gently rubbing your clit and let the other hand gently explore your other pleasure areas…

What are you thinking as you explore your body? What sensations do you enjoy the most? Are you fantasizing about the guy from the coffee shop or about your partner walking in and secretly watching you give yourself pleasure? Are you just focused on how damn good you can make yourself feel?

Lock yourself in the bathroom and run a steamy, hot shower
Hop in and get the nitty-gritty out of the way, if you need to (i.e. follow your usual shower routine). Allow the warm water to relax and invigorate you. While you are washing your body, try fantasizing

about a situation or a person. What if your fantasy man were waiting for you naked on the bed when you got out of the shower? What would you do together? What would he do to you? Allow yourself to think outside of your current life and fantasize about unreal events that are exciting!

A note on fantasies! According to the Merriam-Webster Dictionary, to fantasize is "*to imagine doing things that you are very unlikely to do.*" Just because you think about doing something, it does not mean that you will actually EVER do it. Even if, by chance, an opportunity did come up to fulfill a fantasy, you may not take it. Just because you think it, does not mean you would do it! Often, the easiest things to allow ourselves to fantasize about include people who may or may not even exist, or who are almost never going to really come into our lives (like celebrities), or they involve places or situations that may or may not even exist in real life. Fantasies allow you to take your mind to safe, erotic places without fear of hurting yourself or others. In the deepest parts of our minds, we can create images that will take us on a journey that we may never go on in our current lives. That's totally OK! More on that later…

Buy yourself a dirty magazine or book

Find one that features pictures of naked men or women (or both), as well as some sexy stories. Turn on some music that stimulates you. It might be soft and sensual, and it might be hard and rough … depends what you need at the time! If you can play it loud … do! Otherwise, just keep it to yourself. Turn the light down low or light candles. Lighting is very important; soft lighting is sensual. Read through your magazine … fill your mind with images of beautiful naked people. You will notice yourself feeling more sexual, more turned on. Take this time to touch yourself wherever your body tells you to!

Being able to pleasure yourself successfully is a huge deal. Some of us enter into relationships that are co-dependent or unhealthy, because we feel we NEED someone else to survive and exist. Part of breaking that cycle is finding it within you to be happy with you. YOU DO NOT NEED ANYONE ELSE TO BE HAPPY. Finding ways to please yourself will increase your confidence and your comfort level with being happy on your own. It will also make it easier and more fun to share yourself and your life with other people.

Pleasuring yourself is an extremely effective way of discovering what you like. When you are comfortable with what turns you on (and this is extremely personal for each woman), you will be able to help others give you the pleasure you need and deserve.

You might be thinking to yourself, *Now, wait a minute here, Tina. I am trying to have a better sex life with my partner! The goal is NOT to be doing this alone!*

I know! But if you want to bring out your kinky little self more, you need to know what that kinky self wants: I search myself ... I want you to find me. If you don't do the initial work upfront, you will never be able to allow someone else to find it.

OK, so now you might be thinking, *Great, Tina. So now my once-a-week obligatory sex with my partner will be replaced with me touching and pleasuring myself. I will already be satisfied. How is that going to help me get MORE?*

Contrary to what you might think, pleasuring yourself successfully will not curb your desire for sex. In fact, pleasuring yourself successfully can release your inhibitions and encourage you to have your partner do the same kind of things to you. If it feels that good when you do it, imagine how good it will feel when your partner does it to you! You will be eagerly anticipating your partner's arrival. If you are used to a one night a week escapade with your partner, I would encourage you to keep that date and add in your date with yourself. Try to schedule the masturbation date for earlier in the week and see how the rest of your week plays out. Get excited ... this is how you create MORE nights of passion.

Most of us have to get past ourselves when it comes to masturbation. You may have done it as a child, and then someone caught you and made you feel terrible about it. You may have consistently masturbated as a single woman and then, as soon as you got married, you stopped. You may masturbate regularly to scratch your kinky itch. No matter where you are in your life right now, I want you to ADD 30 minutes of masturbation into your weekly regime.

SWEET, SWEET FANTASY

When it comes to fantasy, you need to give your imagination permission to do its job: make up a story that is not real! While it may not be real, the more you can build the story in your mind, the more you can arouse yourself and turn on the fires of passion in your bedroom!

Just because you think it doesn't mean you really want it … it's a fantasy. I want you to look at fantasizing as a tool that you can use to stimulate yourself and keep things exciting in the bedroom.

You can keep your fantasies to yourself; no one has to know about your dirty desires. They are for your viewing pleasure only. But fantasies can also be used as a tool to increase sexual tension and desire with your partner, if you are prepared to share!

Sharing your fantasies will require that you are open to sharing them, and your partner must be ready and willing to receive your fantasies in a way that enhances your experience. This goes both ways. You must be ready and willing to hear your partner's fantasies without judgment. Communicating in a sexual way must have guidelines and rules, and it is up to you to set these with your partner.

You may not feel comfortable hearing that your partner would like to watch you make love to another woman (or two or three) or to see you being satisfied by multiple men or to use a particular item to enhance your sexual experience. Or, your partner may feel uncomfortable hearing the things you fantasize about. I want to remove the judgment you and your partner may have in regards to fantasies. THESE ARE NOT REAL, and thinking about them will not ensure that they ever happen to you in your life.

A fantasy is usually better left a fantasy. In your fantasy world, there are no consequences associated with anything you do, because it's not real! There are no feelings involved; you won't get hurt, and neither will the five naked Greek Adonises that you invited into your thoughts last night! In your fantasies, you always have the energy and passion you need. There are no repercussions, so you are free to think what you want, when you want to!

In real life, things don't always work out the way you thought they would. They may be better; they may be worse. Sexual encounters are not always perfect in the real world! In your head, they are.

I encourage you to give yourself permission to think about doing dirty things with your fantasy people. Think about things that you would like your partner to do to you, without limits. Push yourself outside of your boundaries. In a fantasy, you do not have to consider any of the logistics that would need to happen to actually make something like that work. You don't have to buy more lingerie, whips, rope, candles or feathers ... you just have to create those things in your mind.

Once you are able to create fantasies, use them to your advantage during masturbation and with your partner. Share them if you like. The more solid your fantasies become, the more you will be able to turn yourself on with them. This will also encourage you to fulfill your fantasies; if it feels that good in your mind, imagine what it would feel like in real life. Use caution here. You know yourself better than anyone. If you want to fulfill a fantasy and you are comfortable with that, by all means do it! You may also fulfill a fantasy and not like it. Look at it as a learning experience. A negative experience will likely destroy that fantasy for you, and you'll have to come up with something more creative to stimulate yourself! It's all good either way.

KINKY CONFESSIONAL

The Day Lauren's Firefighter Fantasy Was Ruined!

I have always had a thing for firefighters … a man in uniform is so sexy! In my fantasy, a gorgeous, muscular firefighter shows up on my doorstep. The reason he shows up does not matter! He is smitten with me, of course, and proceeds to start removing his shirt. He is only wearing his fireman pants, and the suspender straps are nicely framing his chest. He slowly drops the suspenders, and his heavy pants slowly sag down enough that I can see the patch of dark, soft hair trailing a path down to the delight that awaits in his pants. His groin is bulging with the girthy hardness of his huge cock, and he looks at me with fire in his eyes … he needs me to put out the fire this time, baby! He walks slowly over to me and easily lifts me into his arms. Some days, he carries me to my bed, other days to the couch, and other days he takes me on the porch or up against the wall. Sometimes he shows up at my house, and sometimes he shows up at work. He doesn't always look the same … but he's mine, all mine!

When my sister got married, one of her friends organized a stagette for her. The theme: Pirates and Wenches. The plan: gather at her friend's house, watch an amazing stripper, then get dressed in our sexy pirate/wench costumes and hit the club!

My sister's fantasy also happened to include a fireman, and her friend was determined to make that fantasy a reality with a "firefighter" stripper. This was a surprise to my sister, but the rest of us girls knew what we were expecting, and we were excited. It's not too often you have an excuse to have a stripper in the living room! The anticipation almost killed us, but finally the doorbell rang. To our surprise (and horror), the fireman at the door was short, dark, and not all that handsome or muscular. Stifling our giggles, we thought we should still let the show go on! The music started, and our fireman started his show. The uniform did nothing to help this guy's show … he could not dance to save his life, and rather than being stimulated, most of us were laughing our heads off. Once he started removing his clothes, we gasped; his body was covered in a bright, red sunburn. This could not be going much worse. Meanwhile, my sister was getting loud and playful ... and a few hard slaps on his naked sunburned ass sent him running to the bathroom! Once we sent him packing, we couldn't stop laughing! What an absolute train wreck! For years afterwards, my fireman fantasy was crushed. The fire trucks would go past, and I wouldn't even bat an eyelash! I had been ruined by a lobster.

I am glad to report that my fantasy fireman has slowly been resurrected. Now, I steal sideways glances at firemen and see which of them can replace the lobster in my mind. A man in uniform can still do it for me!

KINKY CONFESSIONAL

Josephine's online fantasies become an offline reality.

It was a hot sultry night, too hot to stay inside. I wandered outside with him on my mind. I had never heard his voice or even seen him in person, but the power of his words in his emails combined with the one picture he sent, made me almost faint with desire. I headed toward the beach, and was so wrapped up in my thoughts I didn't notice the figure watching me until I heard a delicious voice gently call my name. Surprised, I turned quickly around and it was him. I don't know how he found me. I stared him in the eyes with disbelief and desire. I wrapped my arms around his neck and kissed him hard. My knees were weak, and I had to hold onto him tightly so I wouldn't collapse. We fell to the ground, and while we kissed I rolled on top of him and rubbed myself on his seemingly large penis. He smelled so good, I needed to taste him. My fingers greedily worked the buttons of his shirt, but my hunger was so strong that I finally tore his shirt open. I kissed and licked his neck as I clumsily opened his belt and ripped his pants down. I took his huge length in my mouth. He tasted even better than I could have imagined. It wasn't long before he pushed me off and eagerly peeled off my dress. The feel of his mouth on my nipples and the slight pressure he made with his teeth almost made me cum. He started working his way down and I was sitting up slightly, so I wouldn't miss any part of this amazing night. I looked down at my wetness and noticed a faint line of blood running down my legs; my period was starting! I gasped and grabbed my dress and apologized. He pushed me back down and started tonguing my clit in spite of it. My cheeks were flamed red with a combination of desire and embarrassment. The exciting location mixed with the intensity of emotions and the fever of anticipation brought me to my peak and I exploded in orgasm. He wrapped me into his arms and carried me into the ocean. We dove in together and when I came up he grabbed me and plunged his thick solid cock into me. His finger was rubbing my clit while he kept plunging in and out of me with his huge length. With the ocean waves crashing all around us, he erupted into me, and sent me to the moon with my orgasm. I had never experienced such intensity in my life. He carried me back to the beach and tenderly put my dress back on my wet body. I shivered as the warm air hit my cool skin. He put his clothes on and we walked hand in hand back to my house. What a great first date!

KINKY CONFESSIONAL

Kristy's Fantasy Surprise

My partner and I had always talked about adding another woman; it was both of our fantasies. He was excited by the thought of having two women take care of him in all the right ways, and he was really turned on thinking about two women pleasuring each other in ways that only a woman could know. Women are beautiful, and while I was very much in love with my partner, the thought of being with a woman and my man was thrilling.

We always talked dirty to each other about this fantasy, and we really started getting good at creating it in our minds. I had a friend who was very sexual and very sexy, in my opinion. We got talking one day about sex and about our fantasies. She told me she found me very attractive, and she asked if I had ever thought about being with another woman. I confessed that I had thought about it as a fantasy, but I never thought I would actually do it. I felt very turned on by our conversation, and it made me wonder if I really did want to fulfill my fantasy.

I discussed the conversation with my partner, and we both agreed that it would be exciting and sexually satisfying to go ahead and get it on with another woman. I asked my friend if she would be interested in joining my partner and I for a night of sex, and she said YES! We planned a night to meet, and I found myself nervously anticipating this encounter. She met us at our place, and we had a few drinks to break the ice. We were sitting beside each other on the couch, and my partner was sitting across from us. When I was least expecting it, she leaned over and kissed me on the lips with a lust and passion that drew me into her immediately. Kissing a woman was great. She smelled good, and her lips were soft and sensuous. I was still nervous, but when her hands started caressing my breasts through my shirt, I could feel myself relaxing and I could feel my pussy getting wet. My partner looked on with a kinky smile on his face.

She slowly pulled my shirt up over my head and gently threw it on the floor. She looked longingly at my breasts and then looked at me and smiled coyly. Then she kissed me some more, while her hands expertly undid my bra. My breathing was heavy, and I was anxiously awaiting her next move. Her hands found my full breasts, and she gently squeezed them with her soft hands. She pressed her body against mine, and I grabbed her tight ass and pulled her even closer to me. She kissed down my neck and onto my shoulders and soon her lips found my nipple. She licked my nipples expertly and sucked them hard into her mouth, while her hands rubbed forcefully at my crotch.

My pussy ached, and I wanted more. I slowly removed her shirt to reveal a beautiful purple lace bra, which her cleavage spilled out of. I grabbed her bra-covered breasts, shoved my face in between her breasts and gently kissed the skin that was showing. My hands wrapped around her body, and I unclasped her bra to reveal her perky, large breasts. Her nipples were large and erect already. I cupped her breasts in my hands and began suckling her nipples.

My partner, who had been just an observer up to this point, came over and began kissing her on the lips. While I was making sweet love to her breasts, he slowly removed my pants and began gently rubbing my pussy through my panties. There was so much going on, sometimes I felt I might lose myself in all the pleasure! My partner took over the job of entertaining her titties, while I removed her pants. She was moaning with pleasure, and it was clear she was ready for more, and so was I. I pulled her pants off, and my partner pulled his own pants off. She began to stroke his penis, and he kissed me roughly. I stroked her panties several times and then pulled them right off. The brown mound of hair on her pussy was soft, and my fingers easily found her clit. She was wet and ready for me. While she stroked my partner's cock, I softly rubbed her clit and then eased my fingers into her hot, wet pussy. It was so exciting to see how much pleasure she got from my touch and from the situation.

It was really getting hot in the room! It was time to take this a little further. I lowered my head between her legs and got my first taste of a woman. Her moans told me I was doing it right. I licked her clit softly at first and then picked up the pace, while my fingers explored the inside of her pussy. She could handle it, so I took the liberty of inserting three fingers into her pussy. I fucked her hard with my fingers while I sucked and licked her clit until she came. Then it was her turn. I sat on the couch, and she spread my legs wide. My pussy was dripping with anticipatory juices, and I was excited to see what she would do to me. My partner knelt on the couch beside me, and I stroked his cock with my wet hand. While she licked me inside and out and eagerly stuck her fingers in and out of me, I sucked me partner's cock and grabbed his balls. We were all getting very excited. We decided it was time to take it to the bedroom.

We had sex with each other for a very long time that night. While my partner was sticking his cock deep inside of her, I would suck her tits or kiss her on the mouth or rub his balls. While my partner was fucking me, she would rub my clit, suck or rub my boobs or kiss my partner. It was very erotic, and I was really enjoying myself. Until my partner moaned and called out her name while he was pumping his cock into her. It had been all fun and games up to that point, and then my emotions got the best of me. My jealousy came out, and the realization that we were having sex with someone else really set in.

Suddenly, I was worried about what we had set in motion. Thinking about my man being with another woman and actually seeing him with another woman were two very different things. I started thinking, "What if my partner likes this so much that he wants to do it all the time?" "What if he thinks her pussy and her tits are better than mine, and he won't be satisfied by mine anymore?" "What if I decide I want to be with women instead of my partner?" The night ended well, and we were all satisfied. I didn't let them know that night that my feelings had taken over. When my partner and I discussed this incredibly crazy night later, I told him how I had felt. It surprised me that my emotions would get in the way of acting out one of our fantasies! While I enjoyed myself, I knew that unless something drastically changed, my emotions weren't ready to go that far again, even if my body was!

Like this fan learned, communication in the bedroom is the key to a healthy sex life for both partners. Read on to explore this topic further…

CHAPTER 3

Communication in the Bedroom

* * * * * * * * * * * * * *

"It takes two to make a thing go right...
It takes two to make it outta sight!"
– Rob Base & DJ E-Z Rock

Communication is key in any relationship, and the more deeply you can communicate with your partner, the easier it will be to please each other. Talking about sex is not always easy. You may feel embarrassed and blush just thinking about talking about sex, let alone doing it! But please remember, this is worth it. Sex can just be sex (which is OK), or it can be lustful, passionate, memorable, satisfying nights.

You need to know what you want, whether you're getting what you want and how to communicate what you want appropriately to your partner.

Talking about sex starts outside the bedroom! Everyone will be at a different place when it comes to communication, especially about these steamy topics. You may feel extremely comfortable talking about what you want to do to your husband's cock, or you may be blushing just at the thought of mentioning the word cock or pussy. Either way, it's time to open up that conversation. It's time to find out the truth and be honest with your partner.

Go out for dinner or arrange for a private coffee meeting or drink with your partner. Being away from your regular routine, with some decent time set aside for an intimate conversation, can make both of you feel more comfortable. Open up the conversation with a simple question, like this:

"So, honey, do you feel satisfied with our sex life? Do you feel like you're getting it often enough?"

Your partner may feel like he is being put on the line, and he may be afraid to answer, depending on how things have been between you in the past. Give him a minute to respond ... just listen and wait. Say nothing. If, after an uncomfortably long silence, he says nothing and is looking at you with fear in his eyes, then say something like, "I was just thinking that I sure would like to have sex with you more often."

This is non-threatening and also inviting. Relax your partner by letting him know you want more of what he has to give.

Continue on with something like, "Would you be willing to try a few new things to help us both get more excited about rolling into bed awake at night?"

I would be expecting a YES as an answer to this question; if it's not a yes, it's time to explore why. You can get kinky, but you also have to have a partner who is willing to go the distance with his kinky girl.

Once you've opened up the conversation and gotten your YES, it's time to talk sex.

Tell your partner what you have discovered about yourself.

1. You have been masturbating and you really like it.
2. You really enjoy it when ... (insert your likes here)
3. You are excited to teach him more ways of pleasuring you in all the right ways.
4. If he hasn't opened up to you yet, ask him again how he feels about your sex life. Then be quiet and listen.

There will always be emotion when relationships are involved. Remember, you would like to see things improve and get more kinky (together). This is not about blaming someone else for your bedroom deficiencies. Having sex, really good sex, takes two people who are interested in making each other feel good.

You may feel like your partner is blaming you. He may say things like:

"You never want to have sex, so I've just stopped asking."

"I didn't think you were into it anymore."

"It's just not the same as it was when we met."

"You're always so busy, I don't want to bug you."

"I'd really love it if you sucked my cock more." (Is it ever enough? LOL.)

As a woman, it is hard not to read deeper into what your partner is saying and start blaming yourself. Men say what they mean, most of the time. They don't usually need you to interpret the meaning; they meant it the way they said it. Be patient while your partner shares his feelings with you. Listen to what he is saying, really listen, and be compassionate toward him. Send him love when you are together, and you will be able to deepen your spiritual connection with each other.

Be sure to thank your partner for sharing his feelings with you, rather than having an emotional breakdown about how horrible things are!

Share your feelings and your desires with your partner openly and you will be able to ignite the fires of passion before you ever set foot in your bedroom. Connect with each other spiritually and mentally, and you will make the physical connection better.

This verbal communication is important! You will be able to express yourselves up front, so when you do hit the bedroom, you will both be clear on the priorities and expectations. Be clear about what you want.

The purpose of this first discussion is to see where you both are and make sure you want to go in the same direction in the future. It's not about where you've been — it's where you're going that matters.

We all have different desires and expectations. You may hold yourself back from expressing your inner stripper because you are worried what your partner would think about that. Meanwhile, your partner may be secretly fantasizing about you as his personal stripper. Connect the two and you've got fireworks, baby!

Learn from your communication with your partner. What does he want? What doesn't he want? Is he willing to go the distance? Is there anything holding him back?

Listen non-judgmentally. What are you hearing him say? Tell him you need him to be honest and that you won't judge or be offended; in fact, you are anxious to fulfill his every desire. You desire to please him and have him please you. That desire will get you everywhere!

Share your fantasies with your partner. Tell him your dirty stories and fantasies, all of the things you might like to try or just "think" about trying. Ask him to tell you his sexy thoughts. Ask him if he masturbates, how often and where he does it.

Get comfortable talking to each other in a non-threatening situation, such as over dinner or when you're driving in the car together. Car rides are great times to chat, and no one can easily run away from the conversation!

Non-verbal communication must also be used and paid attention to. Non-verbal communication — and the interpretation of it — can make or break any relationship.

Being able to read non-verbal cues from your partner and helping him to more easily read yours can be an amazing benefit to both of you, and it can clear up a lot of miscommunications.

Miscommunication happens when you are thinking one thing while your partner thinks something else entirely. Your perceptions are not in sync, and you are not on each other's wavelength. You have missed the point of the communication, which is to have the other person understand you, and vice versa. Everyone deserves expression and understanding in their relationships.

You cannot expect your partner to read your mind, even though the thought of that is really comfy and awesome. It would be great if they could read our minds ... what an advantage our men would have! In time, as your bond grows and you get into a rhythm of effective verbal and non-verbal communication, it may seem like he can read your mind more often than not!

No yelling. Don't hold back. Always express yourself. Be understanding. Be compassionate. Listen and be considerate.

After your conversation, think, "What did I learn? How can that information help me?"

Focus on positive outcomes and ask yourself positive questions. You'll get much better results.

Holding in your emotions is like shaking a bottle of pop and then opening it up: it explodes everywhere!

If you keep it all in, eventually you will erupt. But if you let out your emotions slowly and consistently, like easing open the pop bottle and slowly letting the air escape, eventually the bubbles subside, the drink doesn't explode and the pop is still drinkable.

Think about how you express your emotions. Do you hold them in? Do you slowly and consistently let them out?

It's easy to add new things and feel good when you are able to express yourself and not hold it in. We communicate our emotions and needs non-verbally, even if we don't realize it.

Non-verbal cues can consist of:

- shrugging your shoulders
- nodding or shaking your head
- rolling your eyes
- batting your eyelashes
- sucking your finger
- turning your back
- not making eye contact
- maintaining direct, steamy eye contact
- crossing your arms in front of you
- smiling seductively

Listen to your partner's non-verbal cues and become aware of how you use yours. What are you saying with your body?

EMOTIONAL TEMPERATURE

You can feel energy in rooms and surrounding people, and if you can become aware of the energy, you will be able to use it to your benefit in every situation. I like to think that emotions can be gauged using a temperature scale.

When the emotion and energy feels cold around someone, that person may be feeling upset, sad, stressed, busy, in need of help or overwhelmed. He or she is not giving off warm, inviting energy.

When the energy surrounding my partner or me feels warm, I associate that with feeling happy, relaxed, joyful and calm.

If it's starting to get a little hot around someone, I either sense sexual, fiery emotion or a little bit of anger. Be careful how you interpret these feelings!

Having a sense of what is happening with others by using your temperature sensor will make it easier to live with someone. Anticipating someone's feelings using their body language and their emotional temperature can help you communicate better with your partner, without them having to say anything with their words. If you can sense they need it, a simple hug or an "I love you" can make all the difference. It can also help you decide when would be a good time to bring up the three new pairs of shoes you just bought. If it's feeling a little chilly, I might wait until it warms up before I spring that one on him!

EXERCISE

Emotional Temperature

Notice how the temperature feels at different emotional points in your life. Does it feel cooler around your partner when he is stressed or energetically drained? Is it warm and comfortable when your children are playing nicely and you and your partner are just chatting and relaxed? Does it feel cool or hot when tempers flare? Does it feel hot when you're being pushed up against the wall by your partner and his hard cock stretches out his jeans to get closer to you?

Noticing temperature, even about yourself, will help you assess and manage situations in your life.

If you can keep it warm in your home for the most part, when it comes to emotion, it will be a lot easier to get into the hot and sexy zone with your partner. If it's cold and there is stress or other concerns or worries, it may be more difficult to get into that hot mood.

Men generally have less difficulty letting go of their stress and worries to get their heads into sex, but that's not true for all men. Men and women everywhere handle stress differently.

Be compassionate to yourself and others; provide what your partner needs and try to ask for what you need.

If you're feeling cold (stressed and overwhelmed), give your partner the heads-up that you might need a little more stimulation (massage, bath, etc.) before he gets his hands — or anything else — on you!

While your partner can't read your mind, he can be given clearly defined, easy to follow instructions that will ensure success. It's time to start directing.

Your partner wants to please you. You want to please your partner. How do you make sure both of you are pleased? You've got to communicate.

By now, you've been masturbating and you have a better idea of what you like and how you like it. Armed with that information, it's time to teach your partner how to do it.

Careful here! A man's pride is easily bruised. You must use tact and make it known that he is your stallion, your one and only, and that he pleases you greatly. Give credit where credit it due!

So what if you don't like something your partner is doing?

You have to say or do something!

Don't get mad, don't be mean, just be compassionate and help him do it differently! Show him by masturbating. Say it gently.

Here's how to start directing your passionate time.

Your partner will be excited and more willing to learn something new if he knows that it will please you. The more times or the better he pleases you, the better he is going to feel about himself. He IS a stallion, one who is willing to go to any lengths to pleasure his queen.

Try this approach.

"Mmmmm, baby, that feels good. Move your hand over here, baby." Gently use your hands to move his to the right spot.

"Hmmm, yes, baby. That's the right spot. Now rub it like this, baby." Help him move his hand in the right motion and at the right tempo, and give him more directions along the way.

"A little softer, baby. Oooooh yes, just like that."

If you like it, reward it. Reward him with your pleasing moans when it feels good, and he'll keep it going.

If you don't like it, help him. Don't punish. Teach. Then reward. This is why the "What Do You Like?" exercise is so important.

Keep directing!

"Faster, baby, rub it faster, please! Stick your fingers in me now … but don't stop rubbing…."

"Yes, baby … yes … more fingers … oh yes, baaaaaaby!"

After he pleases you to perfection, flip him over and have your way with him, but let it be on his terms.

You need to be aware of what your partner likes or doesn't like and be prepared to give it to him. Make him feel like he is your knight in shining armor … and that you are going to take care of whatever he needs, so you need to know what his needs are!

Let him be the director. Let him tell you exactly how to do it right. He masturbates. He knows how to love his cock and balls like no one else. Find out what you can do to intensify the experience for him.

Try this approach.

"Hey baby, can you show me how you touch yourself when you masturbate? I want to get better at pleasing you, and I think it would be really hot to watch you touch yourself … I would get all steamed up!"

If he indulges you, prepare to be totally turned on and to learn a thing or two about your partner!

Watch how he strokes, where he strokes. Does he use one hand or two? Does he use lube? How does he lube? Watch him as he teaches you, and when you think you've got his rhythm (and your hands can no longer stay away from his cock), take over and give him a break!

While you are pleasing him, ask him questions seductively to help you please him better.

"How's that, baby?"

"Is my hand wet enough for you?"

"Oh, you like your balls grabbed and rubbed at the same time? How does that feel?"

Let him provide feedback. Ask for the feedback — demand

it even. His joyful moans will be your reward. Ask him to guide your hand and help you with the rhythm and pressure. Remind him that you desire to please him.

Do a little online research on different ways to please a man. You will be surprised, shocked and amazed at how many different techniques there are! Watch a few videos, get a few new ideas and then surprise your partner with them. See how he reacts. Ask him if he likes your new moves. Tell him how much fun you had researching ways to please him. Just by putting your energy into sex and pleasure, you will heighten your bond and ensure that more of your nights are steamy instead of dreamy!

Well, that was a little heavy! Let's get a little lighter and talk kinky communication.

Talking Dirty

You can deliciously heighten your own and your partner's pleasure by using your words. Talking dirty will intensify your experience; it will allow you to release your inhibition and express yourself sexually.

While you are stroking your man, you can use these three simple techniques:

1. Talk to him about what you are doing to him.
   "I love stroking your hard cock, baby... Mmmm, my hand is gripping you so tightly and it slides so easily up and down your shaft."

2. Tell him what you are planning to do to him next.
   "I can't wait to lick your dick. I am going to start at the top and lick down to your balls and back up again until I've licked you wet all over." (Make sure you are still stroking him while you talk to him!) "Then, I'm going to surround your thick cock with my wet lips and suck it down into my throat. Would you like that, baby?"

3. Talk about what you're hoping he'll do to you next!
   "Mmmm, I can't wait until you stick your delicious cock inside me.
   I want you to put it in slow and deep and then pound me, baby!"

You will delight his senses and make him yearn for you.

Our words are very powerful, and it ignites the hearing senses. Any time you can engage your senses during lovemaking, you will heighten your experience.

Tell your man that you want him to talk dirty to you. Soft, kinky words whispered into your ear can make your pussy swell with pleasure.

You can be playful with your voice, powerful, seductive and engaging. Keep each other in the game by engaging with your voice.

The bedroom is the perfect place to have a little fun and really get playful with being dirty.

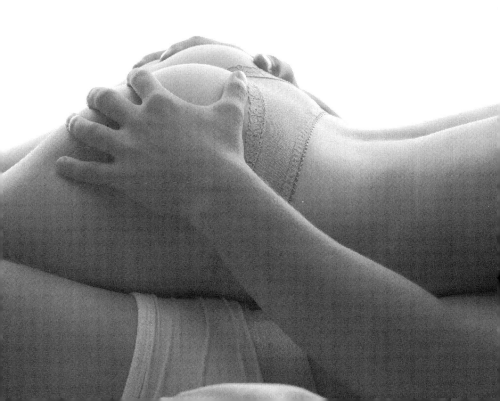

Why do we call it "dirty" anyway?

Dirty, crass words that might never leave your lips in the real world become OK in the bedroom. It's a little role play, a mind game — try getting into it!

Saying dirty words during sex and anticipating next moves will get your mind really going, and it's your mind that makes your body zing with pleasure. Stay in the game.

You can also talk fantasies during sex, if you're both comfortable with it. Remember, they are just fantasies — no harm in thinking or talking about it to each other.

Try something like this (personalize it to suit):

"Imagine if our sexy, next-door neighbor accidently walked in on us having sex and she just stood quietly to the side and watched. When she couldn't take it anymore, she came over to the bed, stood beside us and started unbuttoning her dress..."

OK, so that was his fantasy. And it is perfectly acceptable to tell him a sexy story about something he fantasizes about, even if it doesn't get you the same way.

Now here's one for you:

"I was sitting in my office, typing away, when my secretary buzzed that I had a visitor. In walked the most delicious looking man with a vase of flowers. He had a delivery for me. It was my birthday. He set the flowers down on my desk, then gazed hungrily at me. He closed the door, drew the drapes and lunged for me. He grabbed me up into his strong arms, ripped my skirt up to my hips and tore my panties clear off of me. He gently set me down on the desk, spread my legs and prepared to eat his heart out!"

I could go on, but that wouldn't leave anything to the imagination!

Whatever you're into, use it. Create sexy images in your mind and embrace the pleasure and release that a sexy session can create.

Use fantasies and stories to heighten your senses in the bedroom and keep things KINKY!

You will have your own level of dirty, as will your partner. Communication is key here. If he likes to call you his "dirty bitch" and you just can't stand that, you've got to tell him to stop! If he needs a little more from your dirty talk, he can let you know that, and you can decide if you want to accommodate. Sexual encounters are always about choices. It's not okay to do something that you are not comfortable with.

CHAPTER 4

Feng Shui for Kinky Girls

*"You can, of course, be a sexy,
strong female and be a good role model."*
– Ricki-Lee Coulter

Using Feng Shui to encourage love in your home is an ancient philosophy with origins in Asia. Feng Shui principles encourage you to put focus and energy into balancing the elements in your home and using your home to support your dreams and your wishes.

You are in control of your environment and what you surround yourself with. Our surroundings are outward reflections of how we feel on the inside. It's the inside feelings that count. The really cool thing is that you can have an influence on how you feel inside by taking control of, and managing your surroundings to support your desires.

I love Feng Shui. It is my passion. In its simplicity, Feng Shui gives you the ability to control and encourage positive energy in your home (you want to get as much coming in as you can), and once the energy is in your home, you want to encourage it to stay and hang out in all your spaces.

The yin and the yang, the black and the white, need to be balanced. You need to have a balance of all of the elements in your home. Earth, water, fire, metal and wood should be balanced in all of your spaces.

All right, enough logistics. If you want to learn a little more about Feng Shui, check out my other books, *Be That Girl* or *Be That Mom!* Let's get right down to the nitty-gritty of making your home and your bedroom conducive to sexy, pleasurable, satisfying lovemaking.

At the heart of Feng Shui is the concept that clutter is bad, no matter where it is in your home. Make a point of noting where your clutter is. Clutter will block the flow of positive energy, and it gives off its own level of negative energy. Strive to add simplicity to your life and to your home. Everything in your home should have its own place. This makes it easy to find things and also put things back where they found them. Clearing your clutter can really make you feel calmer in your own home, and it will create efficiency for you and your family. Reducing your stress level can really help increase your desire for love and sex!

EXERCISE

Assess where you are right now in your life. It's time to be honest, and this is important. No matter where you are in your life and in your relationships, you can always strive to do more, have more or be more!

Let's answer a few questions about your passion relationships. You can use the blank pages in the back of this book to write your answers down.

1. Do you have a regular partner?
2. Do you want a regular partner?
3. If you have a regular partner, are you happy with your relationship as a whole?
4. Are you happy with your life and the amount or quality of sex you are having?
5. Could things be better in the bedroom?
6. Have you tried everything and your partner is still disinterested or not willing to add effort?
7. Are you willing to add effort?
8. Is your partner receptive to your advances under the sheets?
9. Are you responsive to your partner's advances?
10. Do you find your partner sexy?

Use your answers to the questions above as a guide to where you are right now, as well as an indicator of where you'd like to go. This is not a test; there is no right or wrong answer, and no score can tell you what you should do. There is no score. This is your life. The only opinion that matters is yours. This exercise is meant to get you thinking about what you have versus what you want and identifying if there is a gap or disparity between the two. Getting what you desire requires that you know what it is! Identify your desires and then chase them. Don't settle and be prepared to put the effort in that will get you the results you want.

OK! That was deep. I am proud of you for answering those questions honestly. Now, it's time to assess your home. There are two main areas that we are going to focus on to ensure that your nights will never be lonely: the front door and your bedroom.

The Front Door — What's Love Got to Do With It?

Your front door is the mouth of "chi" — the life-giving positive energy that naturally flows into and towards areas with vibrant, positive energy. Like attracts like. If your front door has energy flow issues, it can affect everyone in the home adversely in many ways. Here are my essential Feng Shui tips to ensure love runs to your front door:

1. Your front door should be clear, clutter-free and easily accessible and have a meandering pathway up to the door. It should be easy to walk up to the door, and there should be no obstructions. Assess your doorway. Does it feel easy to walk up to it? If it feels good to you and it has good curb appeal, then it has good Feng Shui. Do you have to step over anything or duck under branches? Are there dead leaves, flowers or branches surrounding your door? If so, clear them immediately. Dead stuff gives off dead, negative, stagnant energy and will halt the flow of positive into your home.

2. Add foliage, greenery and flowers in pairs at your front door. These welcome the energy in, and pairs multiply the energy flow toward your door. Real plants and flowers are always the best choice, but depending on your climate, you may choose to add fake flowers or plants. As long as the fake ones are kept clean and look real, they will also attract the good chi.

3. Add a "Welcome" sign or mat. Invite the energy in with open arms. Remove alarm stickers, as these tell the energy to go away and to stay out, which is not what you want.

4. Incorporate the color red into your door area, in your welcome mat or sign, the foliage or flowers or the door itself. Red will attract prosperity and health into your home.

5. Make sure your door handle, stairs and porch are all in good repair. Your front door is the first thing the energy will see, and the appearance here will send a signal about the rest of the home and its owners. A well maintained doorway tells the energy and others that this is a well cared for area and that more positive energy will be welcome and comfortable here. Be sure there is no clutter behind your door; you should be able to open the door all the way and close it easily.

6. Add a water feature or representations of the water element. You may choose to add a fish tank, water fountain or beautiful bowl filled with water and fresh flowers. If adding a water feature won't work here, you may also add the color black or shapes featuring wavy lines in your carpeting or artwork, which also represent water. Water brings incredible energy to your home, so this is an important step!

Who would have thought that I would try to inspire you to get your front door all neat and sweet and inviting to get more kinky?

BEDROOM FENG SHUI

Making Room for Love

No matter where your bedroom is in your home, it is automatically considered your love and relationship area. Your bedroom should be your sanctuary and a place where you can escape the hustle and bustle of your daily life. Your bedroom should be very calming and not have a lot of stimulating colors. Your bedroom is the place where you can rejuvenate, relax and unwind from your day. Sleep is essential for a healthy, happy life, and getting enough sleep can also help increase your desire for sex. Being sleep deprived can add to your stress level, so be sure you're getting your ZZZs.

Follow my top Feng Shui bedroom tips to help you get more sleep and more sex!

1. Your bed must be in the power position in your room. Your bed needs to be in a position where you can easily see the doorway from your bed but are not directly in line with the door. Doorways are the pathways for energy flow, which is good when you want to be stimulated. But when it comes to sleep, you do not want energy rushing past you all night long from the doorways or windows. Keep your door closed at night so that you can enjoy

a restful sleep. Being able to see the doorway from your bed subconsciously puts you in the power position; you can easily see if anyone is coming in or out, and no one will be able to sneak up on you. This is important for restful sleep and also for uninterrupted sex! Make sure the bed is away from the walls on both sides, so that one can easily get in and out of the bed on both sides. Both people deserve to have easy access into and out of the bed!

2. Pairs and duplicity in the bedroom are important. We all want to have someone to share our lives with. Adding pairs of items in your artwork, candles, side tables, plants, lamps and pillows symbolically shows that this room is meant for two.

3. Artwork in the bedroom should be very relaxing and calming. Look at what artwork you have on your walls, and be aware that stimulating artwork could be keeping you from a restful sleep,

while artwork depicting single things or negative imagery could be keeping you from your sex life!

4. Organize and clear the clutter in your bedroom. Being surrounded by clutter while you are sleeping may result in restless nights. And getting in the mood for love may be more difficult for you when you are surrounded by piles of laundry and stuff. You have enough stress in your life; reduce your worries and anxiety by creating a zone in your home where you can feel totally relaxed. Simplify in your bedroom. You should only need to sleep, relax and have sex in this area.

5. No electronics and no work in this area. Electronics give off harmful rays and will stimulate you when you are trying to sleep. Having a TV in your room might seem like a good idea if you want to watch porn, but otherwise, it can adversely affect your sex life. Again, your bedroom is meant to be your resting place and your sexual connection zone. Without a TV, you will be forced to chat with each other, touch each other or just relax. That's the goal for this room. Don't bring work to your room, either. This area should be the one spot where you can get away from work. Too many books in your bedroom can also be very stimulating, so try and keep only the book you are reading out on your nightstand.

6. Add reds, pinks and whites as accent colors. These colors are very stimulating, so use them sparingly in the bedroom to add fire to your love life. Keep your bedroom colors soft and earthy and use comfy, plush materials. The lighting in your bedroom should be soft and warm and still allow you to read when you like.

7. No clutter (or anything else!) under the bed. The energy needs to be able to flow around and under your bed, so when you have clutter under the bed, it halts this flow. Sleeping on top of a mess under your bed can make you have a restless, cluttered sleep!

8. After a death or breakup, get a new mattress.

9. Add plants to your bedroom. Plants are a great way to add life, vitality and energy to your bedroom, and they take away negative energy as well as clean your air. Add two plants to maintain the

sense of duplicity in your bedroom. Silk plants are also good Feng Shui, as long as they are kept clean and well maintained. Fresh flowers are also a great way to add romance to your bedroom. Keep them in pairs!

10. Keep dirty laundry in your closet with the door closed. Dirty clothes will give off negative energy and will serve as a reminder that you have something to do!

11. Balance the masculine and feminine elements in your bedroom. This area is meant to be shared by two, so don't make it too "girly."

12. Mirrors should not be in your bedroom. Mirrors multiply and stir up energy, which is not what we want when we are trying to rest, relax and sleep. Cover mirrors at night if they cannot be removed.

Health	Fame	Romance
Family		Creativity
Knowledge	Career	Travel

13. Remove any paraphernalia, pictures or representations of past relationships. Keeping these items will keep you trapped in the past and will serve as reminders of what you don't have. Propel yourself into the future by releasing the bond those past relationships have on you, and get rid of that old stuff right away.

Now let's take this Feng Shui stuff a little further by identifying the "love and relationship" area of your home.

Standing at your main front door, identify which room is in the far back right corner. This is the area that represents your love and relationships. This may be your bedroom (which is always considered your love and relationship area), but it may be another room in your home. If this area is not your bedroom, the same principles you applied to your bedroom should be applied in this room to stimulate more love and kinkiness in your life. You also have to apply a few "Feng Shui" principles to your body — which you will learn in the next chapter.

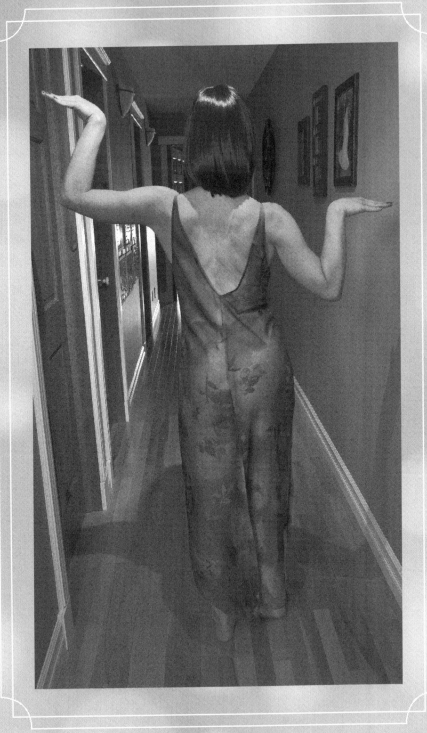

CHAPTER 5

The Egyptian Treatment

*"You can be covered and be very sexy.
It's not what you show; it's what you have in mind,
the way you cross your legs, the way you talk to people."*
– Carine Roitfeld

If you want to enhance the way you feel about your body beyond your thinking, you need to treat your body as a goddess would.

Being sexy comes from feeling sexy about yourself. No one can make you feel sexy; they can only make you feel desire. Your inner sexy can only be released by you. You've been discovering how wonderful your body is. You are beautiful and desirable in the skin you're in, right now. Nothing has to change with your body. You just have to change how you feel about your body and how you treat your body.

Think about how you treat your body. I often wonder about strippers and what they must do to maintain their gorgeous, flaw-less bodies. Do you think they ever get ingrown hairs in their pubic area? How would they handle that on stage? Imagine the care and attention they give their bodies on a daily basis. Their salaries are dependent on how good their body looks, combined with how well they can dance and perform on stage and how engaging they are with their clientele. If your annual salary, health, wealth and prosperity were dependent on your body looking and feeling good, would you change anything about your routine?

I'd like you to think that your "life" salary IS based on your body. Your health and your sex "salary" can all be increased if you treat your body right! It's not JUST about being sexy. It's about caring about you and dressing your gorgeous body appropriately (or not appropriately, depending on the situation).

EXERCISE

Dressing for Success to Get More!

Write down three things you do to your body that make you feel sexier. Here are some examples:

Shave legs
Shower
Wear lingerie
Put makeup on

If you had a hard time thinking of things, it's time to get your sexy on, girl! If you want your partner to treat you like the sexy goddess you are, you have to believe it yourself.

The Egyptians knew the value of taking care of the body and maintaining beauty. They took pride in how their bodies looked, felt and smelled. It's hot in Egypt and not easy to keep yourself smelling great, especially if you have limited access to running water and bathing facilities. Removing their body hair likely helped the Egyptians manage their body odor and probably reduced the amount of sweat they produced. The Egyptians were very concerned with their physical appearances. Cleopatra took the time to care for her body every day, and I think you deserve to do the same!

It's time to give yourself the Egyptian Treatment. Here's how.

BODY HAIR

If you love all your body hair and razors are outlawed in your home, by all means, please skip this section. I am a firm believer that as long as you are happy with your body, you will be a sexy goddess regardless of your choice when it comes to hair removal!

We all have it, and most of us don't want it! I know it's there for a reason, and living in Canada, I understand the value of having hair to insulate from the cold. But it sure doesn't make me feel sexy when I've got stubble on my legs or my pubes are peeking out the side of my bathing suit. Eww!

In North America, extra body hair is not sexy. In my opinion, being silky and smooth is not just for your partner. Being smooth will make you feel sexier. Skin is smoother without the hair.

Being Hungarian, I was blessed with dark hair, and not just on my head. I was always embarrassed at the sheer amount and color of my leg hair, and that stuff really put up a fight! I would shave in the morning and have stubble on my legs by 5 P.M. Believe me, there is nothing sexy about a 5 o'clock shadow on a girl's legs!

The year I turned 10, my mom and dad bought me an electric shaver for Christmas. I cried. How embarrassing! They were just trying to help, and of course, my mom thought it would make me feel more grown up. I started shaving, and I've never looked back when it comes to hair removal. It has not been easy, and I have had some pretty hilarious experiences with body hair.

I have also made some pretty interesting choices about HOW I manage my body hair. When I was in grade 7, it became very apparent after several mean kid comments that having dark upper lip hair was not cool. Our family hairdresser suggested that I wax it. I was so excited, so I took the plunge. It was painful, but I knew it was worth it. I was going to look like a million bucks after this little removal. As it turned out, raging hormones mixed with the hot wax caused a breakout of a thousand little pimples on my upper lip directly following my first-ever waxing episode. Other than the time I peed my pants in class in grade 2, I don't think I've ever been so embarrassed to be at school. What a waxing nightmare; the hair was gone, but it had been replaced by a horrific rash of pimples. AAAHHHHH! I was living a teenage nightmare!

I got over it eventually, and the next time my little moustache needed waxing, my hairdresser turned the heat down, and we used some special cream afterwards. I would still get a few little pimples, but it was worth it. The price of beauty, baby!

There was a time when I was quite happy with the thick, dark bush of hair on my puss. I didn't really know any differently! My "bikini line" grew so far down my thigh, it could have been called the "bikini-to-knee line"! My mom suggested that we try waxing for our legs, armpits and bikini area. I was shaving every day, and just the thought of being able to go a week or two with smooth legs, armpits and a bikini line sounded like a dream come true. Waxing everything was pricey and time-consuming, taking up to two hours! As my comfort level with my hairdresser increased and my inhibitions released, I pulled my panties in just a little bit more and took off a little more hair each time.

When I was in my twenties, I got used to the small "landing strip" of hair, and I decided to take the plunge and go Brazilian! I was grateful that I had such a great relationship with my hairdresser, because removing everything, including the hair around my anus, was a very in-depth experience (asses up, ladies!).

In the past, I had tried once or twice to shave off the entire bush … and that was a process! I don't even recommend trying this at all. The itchiness of that hair growing back and the ingrown hairs were unbearable. There are better ways to go bald, ladies — trust me!

To save money, my sister and I had the brilliant idea of waxing ourselves. How hard could it be? We bought all of the supplies from our hairdresser and excitedly got to work. We had some success and a whole lot of mess! OK, it wasn't as easy as it looked. The legs and armpits were fairly manageable, but when it came to our pussies, it was not pretty. The day one of us had delicate pussy skin ripped open and there was blood everywhere, we decided maybe it was worth the money we were paying an expert to have nice, smooth, unharmed lips!

When I wrote my first book, *Be That Girl*, I started my tour in Toronto. Luckily for me, my favorite cousin gave up a week of her time to chauffeur my un-famous butt all over the Greater Toronto Area. I wanted to be ready for my first-ever TV interview the next day, so we squeezed in a mani-pedi at a splash and dash by my hotel. The lady doing my nails was from Vietnam, and we got to talking about the TV spot. She mentioned that I should do my eyebrow waxing while I was there, to be ready for TV. I figured she was right, so I agreed. While she was doing my eyebrow, she mentioned that my upper lip really could use some waxing. Of course, I agreed. As she was waxing my lip, she just kept saying, "Oh, Tina, look at the hair on your chin." "Oh, Tina, the hair on your cheek."

She just kept waxing and waxing. My cousin was in the room with me, and at this point we were laughing harder than we've ever laughed before. If I didn't put a stop to this hair removal, this lady would go on forever! While I could have felt that she was poking fun at me, in reality, I probably did need the waxing. It doesn't bother me that I'm hairy, and I am not self-conscious about it, but I do make sure I take care of it. When someone else points out your "faults," consider that they are trying to help you! And they are not faults at all; it's just reality. When it comes to hair, there are a lot of options. And let's "face" it (excuse the pun!), I was the perfect customer for someone who specializes in waxing ... the value of an upsell, baby! Just thinking about "Oh, Tina" can brighten any day.

When I started waxing, I was seeking the much-anticipated carrot ... if I waxed for long enough, eventually the hair wouldn't grow back, and soon I'd never have to wax again. Well, those were pipe dreams, and I didn't have 50 years to wait for the hair to stop growing! I was fairly happy with waxing, but the ingrown hairs were getting really annoying. No one wants a huge, painful goiter on her bikini line ... that is not sexy.

(I learned that if you stick with waxing, using a loofah to exfoliate around that area is really important.)

I had heard about laser hair removal, and the dream of permanent hair removal became more of a reality for me. Laser hair removal is not cheap, so I added it to my five-year plan and turned it over to the universe.

Eventually, I was introduced to a friend of my sister's who did the procedure. I was able to get laser hair removal for half-price!

I got laser on my legs, armpits and puss. While I still have some hair growth on these areas, it is significantly reduced, and the hair grows back very slowly. Eventually, I will go back and do a few more treatments to permanently rid myself of the little bit of hair I do have, but I have found laser to be the most effective option for someone like me. No more ingrown hairs, and no 5 o'clock shadow. I maintain my smoothness with a quick shave every few days.

I believe that the smoother we feel to ourselves, the more we will want our partners to touch our soft skin. Removing the hair allows your skin to become even more sensitive to touch ... yours and your partner's.

The only place Cleopatra allowed hair to grow was on her head, her eyebrows, and her eyelashes. Everything else was removed. I am not suggesting that you go that far, but I do want to inspire you to slowly shed some hairy layers.

The first step will be to decide what hair to remove. A trained esthetician can help you remove hair everywhere from your chin to your arms to your anus. What hair do you feel comfortable removing? Do you already remove hair in certain areas? Is there hair on your body that bothers you, but you aren't sure how to remove it?

If you've never removed facial hair before, I would recommend seeing a professional. It is not fair to ask your friends and family what they think, unless you are prepared to hear the truth and not feel badly about what they have to say. It can be easier to hear that you have a unibrow or a moustache from a complete stranger.

Now that you know which places you want to remove hair from, you need to decide which method of hair removal you want to use. There are lots of options, all with pros and cons. Here's a brief lowdown of each one:

Shaving

This is the most popular form of hair removal. It's cheap and easy enough to do yourself. Shaving works best when combined with shaving cream, and it is most effective on legs, armpits and bikini lines. Shaving trims the hair off at the skin level, so the hair will grow back quickly with this method. When it comes to your face, I would not recommend using a razor here. I would also steer clear of shaving your puss lips. You do not want to cut yourself on those lips, and it's itchy growing back in — it can be very uncomfortable for your partner to be rubbed with stubbly lips during times of passion. Plus, if you have sensitive skin, razor burn is a horrible side effect of shaving.

Hair Removal Creams

This is not even a real option. As far as I'm concerned, anything that can "burn off" your hair via chemicals should not be on your skin or in your home. It may be easy, but it's not good for you. The smell is trying to tell you to stay away.

Waxing

Warm melted wax (typically made with honey) is spread in a thin layer over the hair, and then a cloth is pressed down on the wax. The hairy wax sticks to the piece of cloth, which is then quickly pulled off the skin. Yes, it's just like having a bandage removed from your arm. This method is painful, expensive and time-consuming, but you only have to do it every four to six weeks. You have to let your hair grow long enough that the wax can grab onto it, otherwise it won't pull out of the follicles nicely. So you have to be prepared to be hairy for a bit before you go. Since this method pulls the hair out from the follicles, you can expect to be hair-free for at least two weeks (maybe longer if you are blessed). When the hair does grow back, it comes in smoothly, rather than stubbly. If you wax often, you will be killing the roots of some of the hair each time, so your hair will grow back less each time. In theory, over time, NO hair will grow back. The wax is usually not made from natural ingredients, and because of the heat, it can cause skin irritation and rashes. If you don't have really sensitive skin, waxing is excellent for all your body parts.

Sugaring

This is similar in technique to waxing, but the product used is different. This is the method Cleopatra would have used, and it's an excellent hair removal tool. Compared to waxing, sugaring is less painful, and the ingredients used to make the "sugar" are all natural, so you can make your own at home! All you need is sugar, water and lemon juice. Look online for some easy recipes and directions for your own sugar. Just take your "sugar mixture," spread it on a section of hair and then peel it off. The sugaring method is simple enough to do at home, and it yields the same results as waxing; the hair follicles are removed at the root and less should grow back each time. Remember to ensure that your hair is long enough for the sugar to grab onto it. This is a less expensive, less painful option to get weeks of hairlessness. The natural ingredients combined with the room temperature of the sugar make it less likely that the skin will become irritated using this method. Sugaring can be used to remove any and all body hair safely and effectively. Do as the Egyptians did and pour some sugar on!

Threading

This method of hair removal involves using thread in a creative way that rips the hair from the follicle. It is not really as bad as it sounds! This method is feasible to use for eyebrows. While it is similar to plucking or waxing, the removal is more precise, so you can achieve great definition in the shape of your eyebrows. This method of removal is quick, and since the hair is being removed from the follicle, you can expect four to six weeks between threading sessions. Threading is a skill, so this is not really something you can do at home. Threading is painful (as is waxing or plucking), but it is easier on the skin around the eyes than waxing.

Laser Hair Removal

This is by far the most expensive hair removal option, but it is one option that really can give you hair-free smoothness for the rest of your life. Basically, a laser is pulsed over the hair, and that laser reaches under the skin into the hair follicle and kills the root of the hair. Laser is painful (akin to someone snapping an elastic onto your skin), but it's quick! One hit of the laser on small areas of hair and then you're done! Unlike waxing, when you are done with your laser treatment, you will still have hair on your body. The laser kills the hair, but it takes time before that follicle falls out. You will have patches where some hair has fallen out, and some will still be intact. This is not something you want to do the day before you have a hot date, ladies.

Laser does not work for everyone, however. It works best on people with light skin and dark hair, but there are special lasers that can work on lighter hair. Typically, you will need three to five treatments to kill all the follicles, and it is highly dependent on your body and your hair. Seek out someone who has a lot of experience and who is using top-end lasers. If you are considering laser, do your research and do not be swayed by salons offering very low prices on laser treatments. You get what you pay for when it comes to laser. Someone with experience and credibility in the industry is more likely to give you good advice on whether the laser will work for you and is more likely to have higher-end equipment, which is extremely important with laser. If you've got the right hair, laser is extremely effective on almost every part of the body. Eyebrows are a little too precise, so I would stay clear of using laser here. I am sure it can be done, but I'd be careful with my eyes! Be mindful of when you decide to get laser done. Hormones produced in pregnancy or menopause may cause your hair to grow back unwantedly! Wait until you are done having children to get this treatment done, just to be safe. One of my friends had almost all of her hair come back after having her children. What a waste of money!

A good, reliable esthetician will be able to give you sound advice about this. Beware of someone feeding you B.S. If it sounds too cheap or too good to be true, it is. I have been happily enjoying the fact that over 80 percent of my hair just doesn't grow anymore. This is by far my favorite option. But I still shave.

What's Your Bush Style?

When it comes to your beautiful bush, how much hair should you remove? Now that part is up to you, because we all have our own ideas about what looks sexy. Your partner may also want a say in how your bush looks, so feel free to ask his opinion before you launch into something. Cleaning up your bush is a great way to feel sexy and create more excitement in the bedroom.

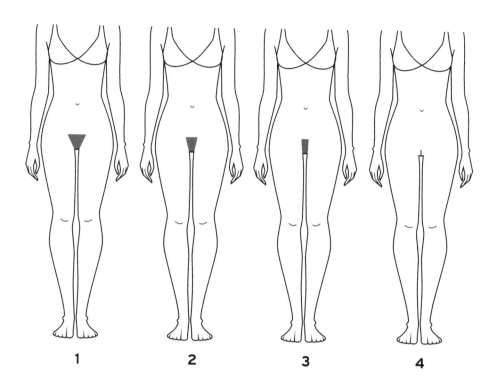

1   **2**   **3**   **4**

Here are a few options:

1. **Natural:** Don't touch a thing.
2. **Classic Bikini:** Remove only the hair that would poke out of a regular bikini-style panty (and anything growing down the leg). Leave the rest of the bush intact. You may choose to trim your bush down a little without completely removing it.
3. **Landing Strip, Triangle or Heart:** Remove everything but a cute little shape of hair!
4. **Brazilian:** Everything gone, including any hair around your anus!

Every salon will use different terminology. A picture is worth a thousand words here, and good communication with your esthetician is extremely important. Feel free to bring your book in and show your esthetician the style you want.

Lady-scaping complete.

Exfoliation!

The next step to that dazzling Egyptian glow is to create more softness on your body. When you are showering or bathing, use a loofah (natural sponge) to gently remove the dead skin cells that can give your skin that dry look and feel. Removing the dead skin cells will help the fresh new skin cells underneath thrive. If you don't have a loofah, using a facecloth to wash yourself will also help.

When it comes to your body and your home, remember to "go natural" and use as few chemicals as possible on and in your body. Organic, natural products are much better for your skin and your body, so start reading the backs of your products for ingredients. Don't know what to look for or don't really care as long as it's natural? Buy products that are organic or natural. For the most part, you can rest easy knowing that these companies have done their homework for you. Yes, these natural products are more expensive, for now, but the more we demand them as a society, the more suppliers will produce these products and the lower that price will be. Be part of the natural revolution, so that one day we won't have to make a choice. The only choice will be natural.

Silkify!

There is the great debate over what to use to moisturize your skin: cream or oil. To be clear, moisturizing with anything will be better than using nothing, as long as you are choosing a natural product, so don't beat yourself up over what you're using. If you didn't know until now that you needed to look at the ingredients on your moisturizers, that's OK. As G.I. Joe says, "Knowing is half the battle." Now you can use the "knowing" as leverage and make smarter choices for yourself.

As a teen plagued by T-zone oily skin and a million pimples, there is no way I would have entertained the idea of using oil on my body, let alone on the delicate skin of my face. Oil was my nemesis! Little did I know that properties of my skin could be used to my advantage.

Faces are a whole different ball game when it comes to the cream vs. oil debate, and it is one that I will leave for further discussion in *Be That Younger Girl* (just kidding!). So let's just focus on moisturizers for the body.

Oil

Oil is natural. It is made from one ingredient: the plant it came from. This is true if you are using unflavored, unscented natural oils, like sweet almond oil, olive oil, jojoba, grape seed or coconut oil. This makes it harder to source and more expensive, when it comes to buying bulk quantities. But you don't have to use much to get great results. Your skin naturally produces oil as a way of moisturizing, so using oil on your skin seems like a natural fit. Oil can penetrate your skin easily, leaving you with a smooth, ungreasy finish.

Oil heats up nice and easy when it comes into contact with warm skin, making it a natural choice for massages. A quick rub of your hands together with your oil ensures you don't catch a chill when you're trying to moisturize your body or heat things up in the bedroom.

Essential oils can be easily added to your natural oils for a little aromatherapy and healing each day. Essential oils are extremely therapeutic, and there are many good choices that can be used for your skin. Some are really good at healing scars or reducing wrinkles, so do a little research of your own based on what you want to focus on. Lavender is a particularly good oil to use for everyday in your moisturizing oil. It is very versatile, and while promoting health and vitality in your skin, the aroma will also be calming and nourishing to your mind as you apply it. Essential oils aren't cheap, and they come in very small bottles for a reason. They are extremely potent, so all you need is one or two drops. A small bottle can last for a long time, and it will turn your bottle of olive oil into a luxurious moisturizer. Go natural and enhance your beauty and focus your mind! I love that. Here are a few good essential oils for skin:

Lavender

Rose

Mandarin

Lemon

Myrrh

Frankincense

Sandalwood

When it comes to smells, trust yourself. Smell each of the oils (most natural stores have sample bottles of their oils), and when you find one that is appealing to you, use that one. If you can't stand the smell, don't even bother. Your body knows what's good for you; you just have to follow your nose.

Cream

Creams are a blend of ingredients and are not naturally occurring, yet there are many creams made from natural ingredients. Creams are wonderful moisturizers, and they seem to form a solid protective layer on the skin. Depending on the cream, you can be left with a soft, smooth luxurious feeling or you can be left with a greasy or sticky situation. Cream seems to sit on the skin and not penetrate deeply right away; it can take time to get right in there. It does a great job of protecting skin because of the barrier that it provides on top of the skin, and there are some fabulous natural creams that "silkify" your skin. Most body cream on the market today comes already scented. Again, I would recommend reading your skin care bottles and identifying the ingredients. Perfumey, long-lasting, strong scents are chemically created and not a great addition to your skin care regime or your home.

There are some unscented natural creams on the market that you could add essential oils to, but it would be a little harder mixing it up, in my opinion. Better to buy natural cream scented with your favorite smell.

Cream doesn't do as well as oil when you are massaging skin. It doesn't seem to keep the smoothness going long enough. I never feel like I could put enough cream on. It absorbs but doesn't keep me feeling moisturized for long. I always feel like I need to reapply cream often to maintain that initial softness that cream gives.

Cream goes on cold, unless you keep your bottle heated or you really use some friction before applying. I do not like being cold, and I will avoid putting cream on at times just to avoid the goose pimples I get while I am applying it! My clear favorite is the oil. You will have your own opinion, and we can still both be right!

Decorating and Adornment

You're smooth, you're soft, you're silky and you love the skin you live in. Now it's time to add a few finishing touches.

While I don't fancy myself to be a high-maintenance girl, I do like to feel girly and pretty, and there are a few more little things that I think deserve some extra time and attention: nails, face and hair (and let's not forget jewelry).

Makeup

Adding a little decoration to your face in the way of makeup is not necessary, as you are beautiful just the way you are. However, putting makeup on can make any night or day seem a little more special, especially if you don't do it very often. When you are getting yourself sexy, try adding a little makeup. Enhance your eyes with a smoky black liner and some Egyptian-style eye shadow and show your partner that you mean business in the bedroom! I am not a fan of lipstick, as it seems to dry my lips out and requires a lot of maintenance, so I don't wear it on a regular basis. But on those special nights when I do add a little rouge to my lips, it makes me feel sexy, and I know my husband likes it. It's a little added punch of drama. Making love and having sex is a little like a game, and dressing up is just part of the game. And you're not just doing this for your partner! When you look in the mirror and see gorgeous red lips and smoky, exotic eyes, you are going to want to pucker up and get your kinky on! Which is what this is all about, right? Remember, you do want more passion-filled nights, afternoons and mornings. Take it!

Remember to go natural whenever possible when it comes to makeup. Protect your face!

Hair

What you do with your hair when you are "putting on the tease" can have a really big impact on how you feel and on how your partner feels, too. Long, dangly hair can easily be used to seductively tickle your partner's body. Pulling your hair up when you usually leave it down can have a dramatic effect in the bedroom, and vice versa; if you always wear your hair up, let it down! If you're not happy with your hair, be sure to schedule an appointment with a stylist and prepare yourself to make a change. You don't like what you have now, right? So if you keep doing what you've always done, nothing will change. Ask a stylist for advice, consult magazines for photos of styles you like and make sure you like your hairstyle. While your hair won't make or break your sexiness, if YOU aren't totally happy with it, you will not feel as good. When you feel good, you will treat yourself well and you will want to add more joy to your bedroom life! Another extremely sexy option is to buy a wig and use it for "special" occasions. Using a wig can be like changing your identity, and dressing up is the name of the game when it comes to spicing up relationships. Go wild and have a few different wigs: the school girl, the stripper (blue hair?!), your favorite actress (Marilyn?) … be playful with your hair! When you're dressing up, bedroom-style, try adding flowers to your hair. Flowers are soft and innocent and sexy.

Nails

Having clean, nicely manicured nails is a must for That Kinky Girl. Nothing tears nylons or scratches your partner's scrotum in the wrong way like a jagged fingernail! And when your toenails leave scratch marks from rubbing against your partner's leg, you know it's time to take care of those bad boys!

Doing your nails takes time, but it doesn't have to take long or cost a lot. At the bare minimum, you should be filing and cleaning your nails once a week to keep the shape good and to make it quick and easy to do. Your fingernails are something others will see every day, and if you aren't taking good care of them, it will send a signal to yourself and others that you don't take very good care of yourself. It's a subliminal message that says, "I'm too busy or I don't care." Show yourself how important you are by making time to care for your body and all of its parts!

Adorning your nails with color is an excellent way to decorate your body and enhance how you feel about your nails. But nail artists beware! Most commercial nail polish is filled with chemicals and will do more harm to you than good. The same goes for nail polish remover. Use your nose on this one and you will soon smell the chemicals that are killing your brain cells, causing migraines and poisoning your body. There are several varieties of water-based nail polish on the market that do not contain harsh chemicals, and these would be a healthier choice if you want to use color on your nails. Unfortunately, these water-based polishes do not have the same rich color or the durability that the scary nail polishes have.

Even scary nail polish does not have enough durability to last more that a few days without chipping, which is why "shellac" and "gellac" polishes have become so popular. These go on like a polish, but a UV light is used to harden the polish onto the nail. It does last, and it looks great, which is why women everywhere are turning to this as a solid option for durable, gorgeous nails. Even I was on the "gellac" train for a while, and then it hit me that this could not be good for me. Not only are there lots of harmful chemical ingredients in the polish, but then you add the UV lights. UV lights are the reason that I do not go to the tanning salons. While the "gellac" nails stay on great, they are a pain to get off, requiring that you soak your hands in acetone for upwards of 20 minutes before they can scrape the remnants off your nails. My cuticles and my fingers started peeling after that finger bath, which was not a good sign. So what else is there?

If you want to have cutesy, girly nails without all the fuss and muss of a salon and without all the harsh chemicals, have I got something for you! They're called Jamberry Nail Wraps, and they're made so that even the least girly girl could DIY!

Check out my website at tinaoconnor.jamberrynails.net to see how easy it is to have safe, beautiful nails all the time.

I always feel more girly when I have my nails done. Pointing at things with a gorgeously manicured fingernail just feels good!

Now that you've given yourself the Egyptian Treatment, it's time to dress for sexual success!

DRESS FOR SUCCESS

Bedroom Style

No matter what you do in your life, you should be dressed appropriately, so that you, yourself, believe that you ARE THAT GIRL, in any situation.

If you work as a lawyer, you've got to dress the part. If you attend a yoga class, you need to dress appropriately.

The same is true when it comes to being kinky. You've got to dress the part, when it's appropriate.

Now, I am not recommending — nor will I ever — dressing too sexy all of the time. That is your choice, and we all want to flaunt our sexiness differently. Do what you feel comfortable with. You may only let your partner see your beautiful, rounded cleavage, or you may sport your rack proudly. Do as you wish and feel good about it.

Start your day off right. Put on matching, pretty bras and panties. These are well worth the investment, and we know that bras aren't cheap!

You deserve to feel sexy and pretty underneath your clothes, and no one has to know about them but you! Coordinating bras and panties are just one of life's girly pleasures.

Who needs fancy lingerie when you can just strut around your bedroom with a pair of heels on in your matching bra and panties? Insta-sexy!

Don't cheap out on your undergarments. These are items you will wear every day, and you will want to make sure they are comfortable and pretty. A well-fitting bra can have an incredible impact on your life!

Let's talk panties. There are several different styles to choose from, and some women will wear a variety of styles, while others will have a clear favorite.

Boycut, sexy stripper style, G-string, sexy granny style and,

of course, let's not forget the period panties. No one gets to see these, and they have to be your most comfortable, ugliest pairs of panties.

There are some extremely sexy underwear out there, so if you're used to wearing plain jane, white grannies, I want you to step out of the box and buy yourself two to three damn sexy panties — ones your mother would gasp in horror if she knew her daughter was wearing. Try a G-string or thong, and if you can't make it through the day, only put it on before you are going to have sex. They will turn your partner on, and you will still be fairly comfy. It takes a few days to train your bum to wear thong (up-the-bum) panties, so don't give up too easily. Once you get used to them, you may appreciate the sexy style and the freedom your butt cheeks have. For sexy, comfortable panties, I have found that the Hanky Pankys fit the bill. They claim to be the world's most comfortable thong, but I'll leave that up to you to decide!

But you don't have to wear a thong to have sexy panties.

No matter what style you wear, they can look incredibly sexy. Panties with lace, bows, ties, pretty colors, designs, ruffles and jewels are a great addition to your sexy wardrobe.

Try on several styles at your local lingerie shop. Pick the ones that make you feel the most sexy!

Make sure your panties fit comfortably, not too tight or too loose. Just right, so they hug you in all the right places.

Dressing sexy is a mind game. Turning your sexy on every day with a little lingerie will go a long way towards feeling sexier, which usually equates to more sex and more pleasure. Pleasure is the goal.

CHAPTER 6

Increasing Your Drive

* *

*"'Sex' is as important as eating or drinking and
we ought to allow the one appetite to be satisfied with
as little restraint or false modesty as the other."*
– Marquis de Sade

The trick of it is to be into it as often as possible — even all the time. How is that possible? Being sexual and being turned on all starts with your thinking.

It is an agreed upon perception in western society that men think about sex more often than women. While this may or may not be true, I would bet that anyone who thinks about sex often likely has more sexual intimacy than those who do not often think about it, regardless of gender. Do you often think about sex? When you are sitting in a coffee shop, do you sometimes fantasize about the delicious hottie sitting across from you putting his hands all over you and in places you can only dream about? When you are at work, do you take mental breaks and think about the passionate sex you had with your partner the night before? Can just thinking about sex make your panties wet?

When I was young, I had a workmate who was one of the most sexual beings I have ever met. She was a woman in her 40s without children. She spoke openly and candidly about her sexuality. She thought about sex a lot, and it made her feel really horny — so horny that she admitted she sometimes had to "relieve" herself by masturbating in the bathroom at work! Believe me, this made going to the washroom a little more interesting for me … was she in the stall beside me? At the time, I could not imagine ever being that sexual! I admit, I was a little jealous of her. I rarely masturbated, even in the comfort and privacy of my own home, and I certainly wasn't comfortable enough to touch myself in a public washroom! I didn't think about sex very much, and that had a direct effect on how often I was getting it. I desired to release my inhibitions about sex and the pleasure that could be attained with it … I wanted to be more sexual and please myself more.

What was holding me back? It was all in my thinking.

How often do you think about having sex?

EXERCISE

Carry a mini-journal with you, and each time you have a sexual thought, make a tick mark in your journal. If you feel inspired, write down what your thought was about. This exercise will help you recognize how often you think about engaging in sexual intimacy. This is not a contest, and you should not bother comparing your tally with anyone else! This is all about you. At the end of the day, before bed, review your ticks for the day and assess your results based on any "activity" that you may have had.

For example, end of day:

Sexual Thoughts: 5

Thought about: ass being slapped; titty grope; a long, romantic kiss; having my partner watch me undress down to the beautiful bra and panties I have on; having the stranger in line at the coffee shop throw

me up against the wall in the public washroom, yank my skirt up, rip off my panties and thrust into me while I try to contain my moans...
Sexual Actions: Striptease for my partner and a beautiful hour of passionate lovemaking with my partner

Sample Day 2

Sexual Thoughts: 0

Sexual Actions: ass slap by partner is rewarded with a long, romantic kiss. Too tired, so go to bed with promise of more tomorrow.
Change your thinking to change your life.

This concept applies to everything in your life, including sex! You have to want it to get it, so how can you make yourself want it more? Know you're worth it.

1. Decide you want it.
2. Ask for it or accept it when it is offered!

KINKY CONFESSIONAL

Claudia Takes It!

The other day, I was changing out of my pajamas and into my clothes for the day. It was a Sunday, so my husband was home, and so were our children. I walked buck naked out of the closet and walked toward the dresser. While I was deciding which sexy underwear to put on, my husband came up behind me, grabbed me by the hips and started thrusting his hips into mine. He was clearly smitten with the naked opportunity placed right under his nose. He was fully clothed, and our bedroom door was wide open! I scolded him forcefully... "What if the kids see?" I proceeded to close and lock the bedroom door. I walked quickly back to my husband, kissed him hard and passionately and said, "At least close the door next time..."

I took my place in front of the dresser, and I leaned forward, letting him know that I was ready to be taken with fire! He grinned with surprise and eagerness. We didn't have much time, and with the kids in the next room, we had to be quiet. His pants hit the floor, and he moistened his fingers with his tongue. One hand stroked his hard cock, while his moistened fingers found my already aching pussy. He pushed two fingers into me and made sure I was ready to accept his gift. Then he plunged his cock hard into me, grabbing my hips and making me moan with pleasure. It was quick and dirty and delicious. No funny business, no foreplay, no problem! You have to take the opportunity when it comes…literally!

How fast can you "get in the mood"? When opportunity knocks, you always have a choice to grab it or not. I would say, if you have a chance to make yourself feel good, take it!

KINKY CONFESSIONAL

Stephanie Sets Up for LOVE

We have been married for over 15 years, and we have young children. Fortunately (or unfortunately), having spontaneous sex these days is not the norm at our house! We are very committed to our relationship, and we always make sure we take care of each other's needs; we just have to plan it a little more. Being too tired at the end of the day is not a good enough excuse … if we allowed that, we'd never have sex! We're tired, but as long as one of us makes an effort, the other one will jump on board. There are times when we get the kids to bed, wink at each other, then run to our bedroom, strip down and jump in the bed.

The most passionate sex usually occurs when one of us puts a little effort into setting the mood. Whoever is inspired that day will light candles in our bedroom and set up some mood lighting. I love to drape a red scarf on top of the lampshades on our room. It dims the amount of light and creates a nice, reddish glow in the room. Very sexy! When my husband looks down the hallway and sees the scarf on the lamp, he knows it's game time. Other times, I will run a bath for my husband, get his book ready and light some candles in the bath. Essentially, I am giving him permission to relax for as long as he needs. We both work hard, and carving out personal time can be difficult with a busy family. These little acts show my husband that I care for him and for us. After his bath, he always rewards me with some passion … even if it's just a kiss, hug and a thank you.

REDUCING STRESS IS THE KEY

There are a lot of things we can do to reduce our stress levels, and one of them is sex. But you can't reduce your stress level by having sex if you're too stressed out to have sex!

If you can reduce the stress in your life, it will positively impact your life in many ways. You will be calmer and healthier, and you'll begin to see your desire for sex increase. Once you feel good, you'll want to keep feeling better and better!

Here are a few great stress-relieving essentials you can use every day to get Zen.

Meditate

Turn your mind over to the universe and reconnect with the life-giving energy surrounds us. Take just 15 minutes every day to sit quietly but actively with your eyes closed. You are alert, but your body is still and your mind is quieted. Focus on your breathing. Feel the inhalation as it coldly enters your nose. Pause at the top of your inhalation and then focus on the warm, slow exhalation out. Repeat. Set a timer, and then just sit and breathe for 15 minutes. Every day. Any time of day. Meditation is very grounding and will make your day seem smoother.

You can quiet anxious, worrisome thinking with meditation, and you can stimulate your mind to come up with solutions and ideas that will change your life. Meditation should be added to any lifestyle, particularly a stressful life. Those of you who simply cannot find 15 minutes each day are the ones who need it the most. I understand that 15 minutes is a lot of time, but if you take it, you will not regret it. You will attract things more easily. We live busy lives, and we often don't stop and make time for rejuvenating and empowering our minds. Some of you may be so stressed out that you feel like you cannot breathe very well. You need to meditate. It will help you learn to breathe. Breathing brings in life-giving, nourishing energy and it removes waste, all in one breathe. Taking time to notice your breathing is important. The deeper the inhalation, the more oxygen you are getting. Just breathing more (and more deeply) will reduce stress and make you feel better.

Essential Oils

Adding smells to your life can reduce your stress. The extracted oils of plants and flowers are extremely potent when it comes to their smell; these oils have been used for centuries in perfumes, and their therapeutic properties are eagerly used for natural healing. When it comes to making your home or your bedroom smell good, essential oils are the way to go. For reducing stress, try adding a couple of drops of a calming essential oil, like lavender, orange or vanilla, on your pillow or bed sheets, just before you go to bed. You can also add drops to a cotton ball and set the cotton ball somewhere close to your bed. You may also use a diffuser or add drops to a bowl of very hot water. Place your head over top of the bowl, place a towel over your head and the bowl, close your eyes and let the steam heal you. Relax and breathe in the vapor. Careful: A couple of drops is all you need. The aroma will calm your mind and help you relax before you go to sleep for the night. Do it a little earlier in the night, and maybe you'll be able to add some relaxed lovemaking to your routine before you close your eyes. You can purchase essential oils at local natural health food stores, organic markets and online.

Essential oils can also be used in unscented soaps to add natural aroma, as well as in spray bottles with water to give your home a pick-me-up. I use essential oils in my front door water fountain and am always treated to a pleasant pepperminty home.

Massage

This one can be the money shot, right here. Massage is so good for your body. Having another person rub your muscles in all the right places, while you lay down and get to relax, is an incredible way to relieve stress. Giving a massage to someone else can also be very invigorating and rewarding. Causing pleasure in someone else is very gratifying! If your partner is no good at massaging or simply won't do it, treat yourself to a professional massage once in a while. It is a whole hour of you time, focused on relaxing your gorgeous body. Your mind cannot help following suit. Use your massage time as your meditative time and just get right into it. Rejuvenate body and mind. If your partner is into it, ask for a rubdown every once in a while. It doesn't have to be an hour massage — how about just 20 minutes? Resist the urge to fall asleep and focus your mind on every stroke and every touch. Where does your partner touch you, and where doesn't he touch you? Think about how good it feels and let your partner know that you like it. After 20 minutes, see how you feel. You may just have awakened your kinky girl, if you can keep her awake!

EXERCISE

Any kind of physical activity you can add into your day is going to make you feel better. Period. Your body needs to move and be moved. When it comes to exercise, try to do things that you really enjoy. Is it the gym, yoga, running, biking, soccer, gardening or walking that "does it" for you? Forcing yourself to do something you don't enjoy just to be active is not the way to reduce your stress. If you love walking, park farther away from the entry, always take the stairs, leave earlier and walk to your destination. Pick a job that has a more physical element or find new ways of being active at work. Just focus on moving your body more often. Taking a walk out in nature is the perfect way to release stress. Breathing in the clean air, looking at the beauty of nature and appreciating the opportunity you have on this earth is an excellent way to boost your positivity.

Get Into Some Hot Water

Immersing yourself in warm water can ease the stress out of you quite quickly. Water nourishes us and soothes us with its healing nature. The warmth relaxes our muscles and eases our minds. Normally, a hot bath or shower can be much needed (and deserved) alone time. Just taking an extra-long bath or shower can change your mood and your outlook on life! Sharing your warm water experience with someone else can be very erotic, cleansing and relaxing, so get into hot water as much as you can.

Assess Your Schedule

Reduce your stress by reducing the amount of stuff you have on your schedule. You may have to say NO to a few things in order to be able to say "Yes, baby, yes" a few more times each week. You have the ability to choose how you spend your time, so create some dirty time.

Sex doesn't always have to be scheduled in. Impromptu sex can be some of the most exciting, invigorating and quickest! I don't care whether you schedule it in or just take it as it comes, I just want you to focus on having fulfilling sex more often. Set a goal, and it will happen.

Ask for help. Letting your partner know that if he helped you around the house more (or helped you with whatever you needed, when you needed it), it would really free you up for other more pressing things (like his dick pressed up against your ass!).

Asking for additional help IS NOT like holding sex for ransom.

Holding sex for ransom is like saying that if he does the dishes, you will give him a blow job (BJ). No dishes, no BJ. This is not a good approach to get extra help. It will work temporarily in the beginning, but soon he'll be onto you, and you won't even be able to use the BJ against him.

When you withhold sex or only give it when your partner does what he's supposed to do, your partner could start resenting you. This is not what we want for a solid relationship.

Asking for help is all in the approach. Try something like this:

"Honey, I really want to have sex with you but I have so much to do! Maybe you could give me a hand in the kitchen so we can get to the bedroom quicker?" (Use physical gestures wherever possible: rub up against him, gently grab his ball sac or wink encouragingly.)

Or, "Babe, I want you in my pants. Let's get the kids to bed together tonight so we can have more time." Add a winky, winky, kinky smile.

Once you reduce your stress, you'll want to start replacing your racing brain thoughts with kinky brain waves.

When you find yourself mentally preparing the grocery list, worrying about the next day's schedule, freakin' out about all the things you need to do ... stop yourself.

Take three deep breaths.

And think about your partner's cock. Yes, his cock. When used properly, it becomes your prized possession, to be treated with much care and attention.

Insert dirty thoughts whenever you can to replace your worries. It feels much better to think about your man's tight ass then to worry about lunches or dinners. Those things will get done, because they have to. Ensure you "get done" by thinking about it.

The better you feel, the more great stuff you'll attract into your life.

Sex Therapy, Baby!

Sex is fabulous stress relief, especially "great" sex that leaves you panting and sweating and sighing sweet breaths of release.

Even not-so-good sex will give you a workout, if you add effort. Endorphins are released, and you will feel energized. I like to describe great sex and the afterglow like an incredible release of tension. You get so worked up waiting to be penetrated and worked over, then you get worked over ... your body stretches and moves in amazing ways, and your actions really get your heart racing. When you are sated and you cum (yes!) or he cums (great!) or you both cum (F yeah!), when you roll over, you will feel an intense release, a calmness and joy that will make you feel amazing.

Start to see consensual sex as a way to relieve your tension, and increase your positivity. You owe it to yourself. Being that Kinky Girl just for you will ensure that your stress levels decrease, and your satisfaction increases!

READ DIRTY, DELICIOUS BOOKS

Taking a dirty book to bed with you can get your juices flowing and get you thinking about how good it would feel to get a little loving. Call your partner over as soon as you need to, instead of falling asleep with the book on your face.

Reading dirty, delicious books will get you HOT! There are many to choose from now, and you can find quite a variety, featuring different topics. Some of my favorite authors are Anne Rice, who wrote the "Beauty" series as Anne Rampling, and JR Ward, author of the extremely popular "Black Dagger Brotherhood" series. These books offer great plot mixed with sensuous sexual scenes that will keep you "cumming" back for more! Here is a special story created just for my Kinky Girls by a local kinky writer, Jean Maxwell. Read her other books, including *The Witch Doctor*, to increase your drive.

MY KINKY VALENTINE

by Jean Maxwell

I met Dee in January.

I call him Dee because that is his first initial. I am Jay, which is my first initial. He calls me "J" in his text messages. Together we are "DeeJay." I thought this funny, so the names stuck. That was 13 months ago.

Dee was the new guy at work, and I felt attracted to him from the beginning. Nothing much happened at first, other than each time he visited my building, he always made a point of saying "hello" and "you look great today."

By October, it became clear the attraction was mutual. He worked out of town, so we began Blackberry messaging, to avoid being tracked by either the network service provider or by our employer. The texts got hotter and more intense. He sent me pictures of himself, including his erect cock, whom I nicknamed "Woody." He kept asking to "see all of me," so on Halloween night I locked myself in my bedroom with my digital camera, a tripod, and some props — a cheapie party mask, black gloves and a costume sword.

I was nervous and had never even taken a selfie with my phone before. Maybe it was the demons in the air, but using the camera's self-timer, I managed to take some outrageous photos. Me holding the sword across my breasts or between my thighs, eventually doing the spread-eagle with the sword across my belly and my gloved hands pressing my legs apart. After awhile I felt a little dizzy, a little crazy and incredibly free. I never thought my hairy pussy could look so ... wicked!

I sent them to him by text, each one more racy than the next. I had tears in my eyes as I pressed send, wanting him so bad yet not knowing what sort of reaction I would get or even if I'd ever see him again.

J: This is me. All of me. For you.

D: Wow baby!

J: Wait, there's more.

D: Ohhh yes, so hot!!!!! God, please spread your legs for me. You are so incredibly beautiful, what a body!

J: Thank you, baby (sobbing, sending the next picture)

D: I'm going to fuck you to death.

J: Any way you want, baby.

D: Gonna shoot my load all over myself.

J: Hold on, baby we'll be together soon.

D: You blew my mind tonight. Thank you…

In February Dee came back to town. We jokingly talk about what areas of the office might be "safe." I scout out the place and come up with some potential rooms. He balks at first, but checks them out and agrees on an empty office on another floor, far away from everybody. He texts me.

D: You gonna pull down your pants and bend over the desk?

J: No I want to say hello to Woody first. Desk-bending later.

D: Pretty sure your panties will be down past your bum.

J: Is that so?

I meet him in the room. A bookshelf blocks the frosted glass window. Finally I have his back against the closed door, and I am kissing him, our mouths wet and hungry for each other. I stroke his face, feeling his late-day stubble against my palm. He undoes his pants and guides my hand down to his cock.

I grasp it, drop to my knees and, no pun intended, go to work. I lick it on all sides, from base to tip, then slip the head inside my mouth and suck it just as I imagined I would all those months we were apart. I massage his balls and caress his buttocks with my hands, then stroke his cock some more. I continue to suck hard and move my lips up and down its length, fucking him with my mouth.

He whispers into the air above my head. "Fuck. Oh fuck. That feels so fucking good…"

I mumble, "Mmm-hmm," and keep going. He tastes and smells clean and pure to me. I take all of him in, let his cock bump the back of my throat. He moans again, but his voice has changed.

"I need to be in you…" he says.

Oh, fuck. Can I really do this? I ask myself. "You sure?" I mumble, my tongue tracing the perimeter of his dick. "You don't want me to take you all the way like this?" I would gladly have sucked him into oblivion, swallowed every silvery drop of his cum and licked him clean.

"I need to be in you," he repeats. "C'mon."

He motions me to the one chair in the room, a standard, padded office chair with metal armrests. He tells me to kneel on it facing the back of the chair, feet together, knees apart. I do it.

He pushes my slacks and panties down, tells me to bend forward over the chair back. I can't see his face. I feel his hand slide between my legs, and my slit is very wet. I suddenly realize he's smearing his own saliva over me to moisten me. God!

I feel his cock press against me, then the head sliding effortlessly into me. I am surprised how neatly and quickly it fits inside. I know it's partly due to his wetting me, but it occurs to me that he's also positioned himself exactly right, for minimum resistance. The word that comes to mind is "precision." He seems to approach sex the same way he does his work ... with confidence and accuracy. This makes me laugh inside.

I feel him starting to thrust. In a few strokes he is all the way in, and I'm loving it. Part of me can't believe it's happening; this is not the way I pictured or wanted our first time to be, but here we are. We're alone, and I have him inside me. We grind together, and he warns me to be quiet. When I start to sigh and groan, he whispers, "Shhh, baby." I can't help myself; his thrusts are powerful, and the noises come unbidden.

He slides his hands over my back, pushing up my shirt. He undoes my bra and squeezes my breasts. He whispers, "Tight little pussy," as he pounds into me from behind. I hope I am everything he thought I would be. He picks up the pace, and I place one hand on the nearby desktop to steady the chair. I try to focus and commit to memory the feel of his dick moving in and out of me, in case I never get another chance to be with him.

He leans over me, his lips close to my ear. "C'mon baby, I want you to come," he says as he fucks me faster and harder. To hear him call me "baby" aloud and in person makes me want to weep with joy. He drives deep, and my body jerks with blissful pain. I want to please both of us, so I reach down with my free hand to touch myself.

"That's it, baby, good girl," he pants. "Make yourself come." I am wet as hell, and an easy few strokes with my fingers sends me over the edge. I can't ever remember coming so hard. I moan as quietly as possible. "Good girl," I hear again, so close to my ear it makes me shiver. "I'm gonna come all over you," he says.

It's hard to form words with him driving into me so hard. "Do it, baby," I say. "Let it all go, baby. Gimme all you got."

"Right … now," he says. He withdraws and places the head of his cock in the crack of my ass, and I feel his warm liquid flowing over the skin of my cheeks and pooling in the small of my back. I hear him breathing hard, like he's just run a marathon.

I don't want to clean up; I want his cells and his scent all over me for as long as possible. I reach around and gather a handful of his precious cum in my hand. He steps back from the chair, and I straighten and climb down off it. I turn to him as he stands there with his pants around his ankles.

I lean toward him and swath our combined juices across his lips. They glisten in the greenish fluorescent light from overhead. His brown eyes go wide with surprise. "This is us, baby," I whisper, bringing my mouth close to his. "Taste us together."

I kiss him, our essences passing between us, and our lips slipping and sliding against each other in the slick product of our lovemaking. We taste of salt, of bread, of cinnamon and vanilla. So sweet.

I want a picture of us, so I snap one with my Blackberry. Not a great shot, but something to remember this day by.

It is February 14th.

Dee finds his voice. "J. That's the best Valentine's Day present ever."

THE END

"Sexting"

Part of the thrill of sex is the lead up and anticipation of it. Before cell phones, one could easily write a sexy note and deliver it to their partner, though it may have taken a little longer to get to the person! Nowadays, it takes just seconds to type up a deliciously hot note and send it to your beloved. Use texting as a way of telling your partner what you want him to do to you and also what you would like to do to him. You can take sexy pictures of yourself naked, the panties you selected for the day (the ones they will get to see in person very soon) or one of your body parts. Be creative! Trying to take a sexy "selfie" is not easy, but it will be worth the effort. You will be turned on thinking about how your partner will react to your text, and your partner will be turned on when he receives it. The anticipation will make the act even more delicious.

READ OR WATCH PORN

All of our senses contribute to our thoughts and our body's reactions, when it comes to sex. Reading or just looking through a dirty magazine can be an easy way to get yourself in the mood, and it can also enhance your experience with a partner. While a magazine uses your visual senses to get hot, watching a porn movie will use your vision and your hearing to take you to the next level. Watching and listening to other people having sex is very exciting and can turn you on very quickly. The nice thing about owning a porn mag or video is that you can reuse it over and over again to stimulate yourself in sexual ways. Whether you use it alone or with a partner, you may only get through part of your movie before you are so turned on that you need to relieve yourself(ves), so you won't really get bored watching these over and over again.

EXERCISE

Buy yourself a porn mag (magazine filled with pictures of naked or almost naked people, as well as sexy, erotic stories). These can be found in most convenience stores. If you've never bought one before, you might feel a little embarrassed or excited. Pick one that appeals to you, which may be one with mostly naked men, only naked women, or a combination. There will be ones that offer sensual pictures, and there will be ones that offer more dirty combinations — classy or rough, you may want to buy a couple to see which ones you like. Unlike Cosmo and People magazines, these are usually wrapped in plastic, so you won't be able to browse them in advance of purchasing, but the covers will tell you a lot about what you'll find inside. As far as selection goes, you will notice a focus on naked women, as men have typically been the ones to purchase these magazines. Take your magazine home and find a quiet spot to peruse your new purchase. See how you feel after you've looked at all the pictures. These magazines will also have a few stories in them. Read them sexily to each other or yourself to heat up your bedroom.

EXERCISE

Buy yourself a porno movie. Your local sex shop, which I will discuss soon, will be a great place to find a decent movie focused on sex. When you are looking for a movie, be sure to read the back. The back of the movie will show you what to expect from each movie, using mostly pictures and some text. You will be able to find porn movies that focus on lots of different fantasies, fetishes, genders and positions. Some are lighter in style and will focus on male-female interactions. Others will focus on many women with one man, many men with one woman, women only, men only … you name it, and you'll be able to find it. If you're looking for porn with gorgeous, delicious men in them, I wish you luck.

Again, men are the principal target market for these movies, so you will notice a focus on beautiful women, and the camera will focus on the woman, as well as what is being done to the woman! As far as the men are concerned, you will notice a focus on assets other than his good looks ... size and stamina matter more than tall, dark and handsome when it comes to porn! You can learn a lot from watching porn, but remember that these people are professionals! What they make look easy may take extra prep work behind the scenes that you don't see, and a lot of positions are done specifically to get good camera angles, rather than for pleasure. Don't expect a whole lot of plot line with these movies. Many are plays on real movies or shows, with similar names and farces on the plot, like "Down Town Abby," "X Rated Men" or "Aladdin and the Magic Cock," while others leave nothing to be discovered by their titles, like "Gangbang Party #28" or "Anal Invaders."

Choose one or two that appeal to you. Once you've watched a couple, you'll know what to look for in the future. Yes, some of them are super cheesy, and some are very classy. There are porn movie awards, similar to the Oscars, so if you see one that boasts an award, it may be a smart choice, but it depends what category they won the award for! Have fun with this, and use it to learn and get horny!

Of course, you also need a willing and enthusiastic partner — so read on to learn how to turn him on ... and turn yourself on at the same time.

CHAPTER 7

What Men Really Want
(And How to Be That Girl)

· ·

*"When you feel sexy or sensuous,
you naturally want to open up and give,
and I think that comes from being
able to receive love and desire."*
— Demi Moore

What do men really want?

Adding to my rant about strippers … do you think strippers have more sex? I don't know the answer, but I think the question is interesting.

The profession known commonly as "stripper" or dancer has been around for centuries. Women (and men, too) put themselves on display and perform in clubs to earn a salary. They dress up in costumes and then sexily dance on a stage in front of an audience, and they create a show of removing their clothes. Men are willing to pay to see these shows, and there are many "gentlemen's clubs" in most cities around the world. These clubs are not (generally) places where men can pay to have sex; these are clubs where men can socialize and be turned on by beautiful women who are more than happy to display their sexiness.

These dancers are the epitome of a man's vision and fantasy of the perfect woman, which is why you see such a variety of women on the stage: large breasts, really large breasts, small breasts, curvy, skinny, long hair, short hair, dark skin, light skin, tanned or pale, younger or older. While men may find all of the women beautiful, each will have their own taste when it comes to women. Why do you think that men are so attracted to these women? In my opinion, one reason is that they are the ones putting themselves out there. Two, they take very good care of their bodies, they treat their bodies like shrines and they're not scared to put it out there. They have confidence in their bodies and they put focus on their hair, their nails, their clothes and their weight. A lot of women who aren't strippers do this, too! What I am trying to get at is men want you to flaunt your stuff more around the house! Be more confident in your body and treat your skin and your self with care. When you love yourself, you take very good care of you, and it shows.

Remember, men don't see your stretch marks or your saggy boobs ... they see something delicious that they can get right into! As long as you're into it, they'll be into it, too.

PROSTITUTION

Did you know that prostitution was the very first "career"? Dating back to ancient times, paying to have time with a woman is the oldest profession in the world! Recently, I visited the amazing ruins of Ephesus in Turkey. Here, I witnessed one of the first advertisements: a stone carving telling visitors to the city where to go if they were of age and lonely.

It was really amazing to see this with my own eyes, but it was not very surprising. Sex is pleasurable, for both women and men, and men are prepared to exchange money for this valuable service. I want you to realize what a valuable service you hold in the palm of your hands (and between your legs!). As a woman,

you are in control. You have the key, and men want to unlock your secret box as often as possible. It is incredibly interesting to me to ponder this fact.

If we, as women, begin to use our power and control in this area for our own benefit, we can rule our land, as Cleopatra once did. You will make love, have sex and romance your man because you want to please yourself and please him. How rewarding is it for you to know that you hold the key to your sexual happiness, as well as your partner's? Your man wants more sex from you. Not because he is a pervert. He is a man. Looking at this from a purely anthropological sense, men's bodies and minds have been designed to procreate. We are animals, in the strictest sense of the word. As animals, from a purely genetic standpoint, it is the goal of a human to carry on his or her genes and keep the human race going. Men are good to go more of the time than women are. Women can only procreate every nine months and produce offspring. Men can spread their seed often! The more they spread their seed, the more their genes will carry on. This is just a genetic, ingrained fact.

Our societal norms tell us that this is not necessarily acceptable; being promiscuous as a man for the good of the human race wouldn't necessarily gain you any points with the women of today's world! But it is interesting to consider this fact and realize that men and women are created with a specific genetic goal in mind: carrying on our race.

KINKY CONFESSIONAL

Stacy's Hotel Surprise

It's so exciting planning different ways to keep our sex life interesting. I love surprising my partner and keeping things interesting and sexy. It's not always about the sex; the lead-up to it can be just as exhilarating. One day, I took our passion play to a new level. It was a Friday morning, and during my coffee break at work, I drove to a reasonably priced local hotel and booked myself in. I got two keycards and headed back to work. On my lunch break, I drove to my husband's work and left an envelope addressed to him, labeled private and confidential. Inside the envelope, I put the keycard to the hotel and a note written on the hotel's stationery that said, "Meet me at 6:30 in room 808. -Your Secret Admirer."

I made sure to get off work a little early, as I had a few stops to make on the way. I had arranged with a florist to prepare some fresh flower petals for me, and I stopped to get wine, cheese, fruit and chocolate. Once I got to the hotel, I turned on some romantic music and sprinkled flower petals on the floor from the door to the bed and from the bed to the bathtub. I also put a few petals on the bed. I prepared the food on a serving tray and placed it on the bed, and I opened the wine. I lit the candles I brought from home, ran a nice hot bubble bath and got into my sexiest lingerie. I was extremely aroused and excited, and I had been all day!

The anticipation of surprising him and then spending an

amazing night with him was really exciting. I was pacing the room waiting for him to arrive. I lay on the bed to wait. I gently massaged my breasts, and soon my fingers were sneaking into my bra for a little rub. A few strokes of my nipples, and my pussy was throbbing and wanting to be touched. I wanted to wait for him, but he was late, and I was horny! I slid my beautiful pink panties to the side, moistened my fingers, and began to gently rub my clit. I closed my eyes and was soon into a rhythm that could not be stopped. It felt so good, and I was imagining all the things my husband was going to do to me when he got there. I gave myself a lovely orgasm, and when I opened my blissful eyes, I saw my husband leaning up against the wall watching me with a sly smile and two very hungry eyes. The food and the bath might have to wait!

While I had planned out a romantic night, the unplanned masturbation ended up being a highlight for both of us and a memory that neither of us will soon forget. Needless to say, we talked, we screwed, we ate, we drank, we bathed, we screwed some more and we slept like babies. What a treat to spend a whole night dedicated to pleasing each other in all sorts of ways, and doing it in a place away from the routine of home made it easier to ignore the day-to-day responsibilities that were awaiting us there and have the freedom to be as loud and dirty as wanted to be, for a night.

You're never fully dressed without your kinky smile! Playful, secretive, seductive and sexy, your smile can say it all. As can your eyes. When you are in the mood, there is a heat that emanates off your body like steam, and your eyes can scream, *Take me … take me now, or I will be forced to jump on you and throw you down on the bed and take you myself!*

DRESSING UP IN THE BEDROOM

When you want to bring on the sexy in your bedroom, you've got to put some effort into your costume. Dress for sex-ess!

I know that your pajamas are comfy and cozy and make you

feel good, but your jammies aren't going to make you feel kinky. My husband and I joke about me "putting on my lingerie" when I'm really getting my PJs on. I'm sure he would rather I was putting on real lingerie, because we both know full well pajamas can have the opposite effect of lingerie — sleepy time anyone?

Lingerie or bedroom attire is not always the most comfortable, but you've got to take some comfort in that! Lingerie doesn't usually stay on for too long, and if it's being used properly, you won't have time to think about how your clothes feel.

Taking the time to get dressed into something sexy for yourself or your partner puts intention into your outfit: you mean business, and it's about to get hot in here.

Unlike the comfy safety of your jammies, lingerie makes you stand taller and demand recognition and attention. No chance of falling asleep once you've got your sex attire on — not until the lingerie is safely deposited on the floor and you are breathing the sweet sighs of satisfaction!

Contrary to what many women complain about, lingerie is not just put on to please your partner. Sex is not one-sided; both parties need to be interested and involved. Donning one of your sexy negligees tells your partner that you are ready to play, and it gets them into the game quick. Lingerie is for both of you. You do want more good sex, right?

Let's not deny it. Men love lingerie. There is nothing sexier for a man than having his woman strutting the length of their bed in lacy, sheer revealing materials. While no matter what you wear, if you are confidently strutting it with that sexy look in your eyes, your man will be turned on! Lingerie highlights the sexy, beautiful parts of a woman, and the promise of unwrapping that beautiful gift is exciting for men! Women are beautiful.

Put yourself on display for your partner. You are here to be pleased and give pleasure.

I recommend you take your partner lingerie shopping.

COSTUMES

Lingerie is not the only thing you can wear to heat up your bedroom. Dressing up in other costumes can be a real turn-on. This is where you get to have a little fun. Think of it like this: When you were a child, you played, just for the sheer pleasure of playing. How much do you "play" in your life now? Do you feel that you deserve to have time to play? (The answer is YES.)

This is your time to have fun. Pretending to be something or someone different is exciting and playful. Remember, it's a game, so play it!

Start collecting a "tickle trunk" of items you can use for bedroom dress-up, and you can role play your fantasies with your partner.

Ask your partner what he would like to see you dressed in. What are his favorite "costumes"? Don't judge. If your partner tells you he really loves Cher and wants you to dress like her, go for it and don't ask why. Don't be jealous of your partner's fantasy lovers. You have a set of your own, and it's all good. It's not real; it's just theater for your mind.

Make sure your costume is sexy or can be made sexier. My rules of thumb for a good costume:

1. Keep the skirts short.
2. Ensure there is a lot of cleavage.
3. Make sure it's not easy to take off – this makes the strip much more exciting!

Here are a few popular costume ideas:

For Her:

- Stewardess
- Pirate wench
- Schoolgirl
- Baby
- Stripper
- Dominatrix
- Police officer
- Maid
- Vampire
- Bunny
- Cowgirl
- Cheerleader
- Famous actresses/singers/etc.
  – a little Marilyn

For Him:

- Fireman
- Pilot
- Police officer (make sure you have handcuffs)
- Tarzan
- Biker (wearing only his leather chaps)
- Cowboy
- Pool boy
- Pizza delivery guy
- Army/military
- Rico Suave
- Pirate
- Ninja
- A famous actor/singer/athlete who does it for you
- Vampire

Adding a wig to any outfit will be a delight for you and your partner. Changing your look can make you feel a little different, perhaps even release a little of your inhibition. You don't have to be a "bad girl" to be kinky ... but it wouldn't hurt.

Pushing yourself out of your comfort zone a little is important; it means you are exploring, growing and learning. With that in mind, are you ready to get down to business?

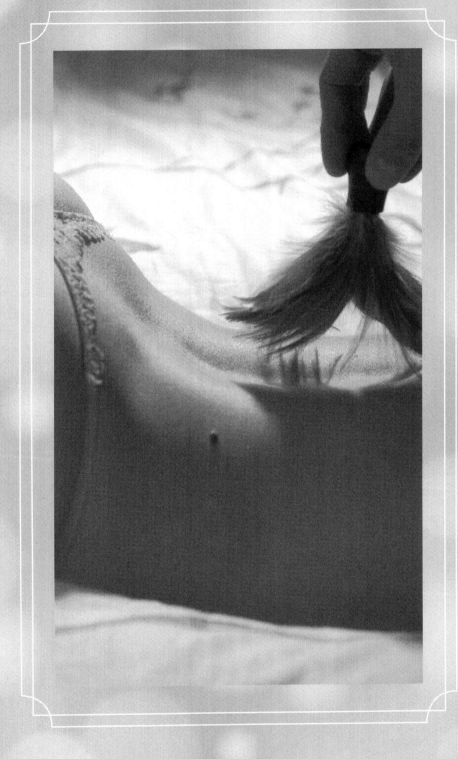

CHAPTER 8

The Act:

How Will You Know You Have Succeeded at Sex?

* * * * * * * * * * * * * * * * * * * *

"Lust is what keeps you wanting to do it even when you have no desire to be with each other. Love is what makes you want to be with each other even when you have no desire to do it."
– Judith Viorst

As long as you feel good after any steamy session, then you've done it right!

How important is it to cum, or orgasm? Very. For both men and women. That intense feeling is what we strive for, and women everywhere want to orgasm more! What does it mean to cum, or orgasm? For men, it's very easy to identify when they have reached orgasm. Hot, juicy lava flows out of the tip of their penis; it's kind of hard to mistake, so you'll know that your man reached the heights of his potential and been fulfilled in one way.

The act of "cumming" is not necessarily as easy to detect when it comes to women, for either party involved. For men, it can especially difficult to know if he has pleased his partner. How will your partner know that you have been satisfied?

There are some women who "squirt" when they cum, but not everyone does. A man who has only had sexual partners who do "squirt" when they come may feel like he hasn't satisfied you if you are not one of the women who squirt upon orgasm. He just doesn't know any better, so reassure him whenever you can that you are satisfied.

What does it mean to cum for a woman? What should it feel like?

We experience an orgasm when we feel an extreme pleasure from a particular stimulation being done to our bodies. The intensity reaches the erupting point when you feel as though you might never return from that delicious space and then you erupt at the top and begin your descent down from the mountain of pleasure.

There are several ways for a woman to reach orgasmic pleasure, and each woman will require different stimulation to reach their peak; each woman will like a variety of different things depending on the day, or hour of day!

This is why communication in the bedroom is so important: moaning loudly when you really like it, using verbal encouragement, using actions like grabbing his head or hands and holding them in place or grinding up to meet him as he pounds you. Your man won't be able to get you to the top of the mountain without a little help.

Do you ever do anything during sex that you're not proud of? Like farting or pussy farting? Remember, sex isn't meant to be clean. That's why we call it dirty! We are dealing with the human body, so don't be embarrassed. Be prepared for anything. A little fart can make you both giggle, but try not to let it be a turn-off. If you did the fart, just smile shyly and keep it rolling. Don't make a big deal out of it. If your partner did the fart, be compassionate.

You are pushing into some pretty exciting territory, but when your legs are squeezed up to your chest and your stomach gets squeezed, you just might have to fart. It's all good.

BREAST AND NIPPLE STIMULATION

Having your breasts and nipples played with exclusively can really get things hot and juicy between your legs. Your nipples may be so sensitive that, if played with in the right ways, you can be brought to orgasm without anyone touching anything else. Men love boobies. Big ones, small ones … it really doesn't matter. If they get to touch them, suck them, bite them, have them squished around their cock, they'll take them. Let your partner get a little kinky with your breasts!

BOOBIE EXERCISE

I challenge you to try to have an orgasm just by stimulating your beautiful titties. It might be your own touch that brings you to your peak first, but challenge your partner to try and make you cum with a good boobie screw. No touching anything else, just pure focus on your girls.

Little nibbles; gentle, pinching, long, hard sucks on the nipples; quick, flitting licks; or a soft, wet cock tip rubbing all around your titties and your nipples — it's time to give your boobies the attention they deserve, and you will both be rewarded.

CLITORAL STIMULATION (AHHHH, THE CLIT)

Just writing this book, I can feel my labia swelling with extra blood flow, and my clit starts to scream for attention. You can literally FEEL yourself getting turned on.

Imagine how much desire your pussy is going to feel while your titties are getting all the action. It's been begging for it, and now you're ready. Your clit is like a tiny, little secret pleasure zone. If touched in just the right way, you will be begging for more, and more, and more!

Your clitoris is at the top of your vagina, inside the lips. It has been fondly referred to as the female penis, since it becomes erect when it is stimulated. There are an incredible amount of nerves ending at your clit. It is an extremely pleasurable zone and one that you should actively explore by yourself and with a partner.

If you've already been working your boobies or you've been fantasizing and thinking about sex, your juices will be flowing and will provide a nice, natural lubrication you can use for some clit play. Moisten your fingers with your own juices, your saliva (or your partner's) or a lubricant.

A note on lubricants: Always use water-based, natural lubricants if you are purchasing them at the store. Water-based lubricants will react more naturally with your body, and there will be less chance of irritation. You may also use coconut oil as a natural, smooth and tasty lubricant.

Some women will need more lubricating than others. This does not mean that you are less turned on than someone who generates more natural lube. Depending on hormones and genetics, you will just need the appropriate amount for you. Things should always glide smoothly and easily. If you feel any friction or feel like things are "sticking" going in and out, add some lube! Don't be embarrassed to ask to be lubed up. Your partner will enjoy making you wet in all kinds of ways. The wetter you are, the more enjoyment you will have. Saliva is a great lubricant, but there are lots of other options, too.

You may not even have to ask to be lubed up, especially if you keep it close at hand. Just hand the lube over to your partner with a kinky wink or smile when you know you need it. A well-oiled machine just works better.

Clit! Since you've been working on yourself each week, you should have a firm grasp on what works for you when it comes to stimulating your clitoris. Usually, you need to ease the clit into a vibrant state: gentle, moist strokes to entice it into standing at attention, followed by firmer, more rapid strokes, interlaced with gentle moistness until you reach climax.

It is normal for your clit to feel extremely sensitive after you orgasm. Make sure your partner is aware of this and that post-orgasm clit stroking needs to be soft, smooth and easy going, until you are ready to get heavy again!

When you are riding your partner and you are on top, you will be able to stimulate your clit when you move back and forth on his cock. You will be in control of how much and how fast you stimulate yourself when you are on top, so use your clit! Also, when your partner is on top, feel free to moisten your fingers and rub your clit to perfection, or encourage him to do it for you. Clitoral stimulation can produce intense orgasms, and it is the easiest area to focus your energies on. You will be rewarded most often using your clit.

If your partner is taking you from behind, this is also an optimal time to rub your clit. Add pleasure to your pleasure!

The clit is key, so be sure you are getting what you want when it comes to this. Command your partner gently:

"Softer, baby, oooh yeah, gently."

"Faster, baby, please rub it faster, oh yeah, harder, baby, yes! Don't stop … yes, yes, yes … ahhhhhh!"

"It's so sensitive now, baby. Just pet it gently and add some moisture… Mmmm. Yeah, that's good."

Providing feedback and encouragement will help both you and your partner. Desire to please each other and you will always succeed.

THE "G" SPOT

We've all heard of it, but many of us have not yet discovered this hidden erogenous zone. Men strive to find this hidden treasure of pleasure; if only they had the key, they would be kings! A man wants to please you. It is his desire. He is proud and happy when he has properly fucked your brains out. He has done his job!

Where is it, and how does one find it?

Supposedly, this zone is located at the back of the vagina and up a little. Insert your fingers into your pussy as far back as they can go, and then bend your fingers up. Once you get your fingers in that position, stroke them back and forth and see what happens! You can also tell your partner to go in search of this erogenous zone. Some women are easily able to have a G-spot orgasm, while others keep searching for a treasure that may never be found. Do not despair if you and your partner never find it. Let the search itself be the pleasure and the goal.

There are special "toys" you can buy, designed to stimulate the G-spot area.

Rock his Cock

The Blow Job and the Hand Job

You may have already perfected your hand and blow job techniques, but this is the perfect time to practice your communication skills in the bedroom. Ask him to help you turn him on even better than you already do! You do not have a penis, so knowing what to do to it to produce intense pleasure can be difficult. And just as with a woman, every man will have his own favorite things when it comes to his cock. What matters here is that you make him feel like his cock is king. Worship his cock, and you'll please him every time. Here are my top tips to give the perfect hand job:

1. Moisten your hand with saliva or use a natural lubricant. Start slow. Grab his cock lovingly and start stroking it slowly up and down. Make sure you have enough lubricant so your hand glides easily up and down his shaft.

2. Use your other hand to gently stroke his ball sack. Moisten your hand for this job also. Gently squeeze his balls and try gently

pulling them. (Remember to gauge his reaction when you do something different ... does he like it? Be sure to ask and watch his body language.)

3. As you are stroking his cock, use different levels of pressure. Squeeze a little harder and intensify the experience. Keep it light and softly stroke the sensitive tip of his cock.

4. Increase the speed. Keep the lubrication going – you do not want to be rubbing fast without lubricant!

A great hand job can make him cum! If you're too selfish and want to make sure you get some this time, slow it down before he erupts and then take yours.

Now is the time to give your man a good blow job; put his cock in your mouth and take him to the next level. Most men absolutely love blow jobs. The pleasure you can give him with your mouth is intense, and he will thank you for it and beg for more if you do it right. Taking a man's cock into your mouth is highly erotic, but for some women, it can be a bit much. You may worry about cleanliness or gagging on his length. I would implore you to change your thinking about this. If you are worried about cleanliness, ask him kindly to wash himself right before you do the deed. Most men would do almost anything to have you take them deep into your mouth. The warmth and wetness of your mouth is very inviting and feels very much like your pussy, but different! Remember to worship his cock. You can make your man feel powerful just by sucking his dick. You may be totally appalled by the idea of taking him into your mouth. If it's a bit much for you to even think about putting his dick in your mouth, just take it slow. Think nice thoughts about his cock, how smooth and soft the outside is, yet how powerful and hard it is when it thrusts into you. The hardness is for you. The blood is flowing into his shaft because he wants you. Love his cock, and he will reward you by pleasing you in the all the ways you want!

Here are my top tips for giving an amazing blow job:

1. Moisten your lips with your saliva and gently take his tip into your mouth. His penis is very sensitive at the top, so don't be too gentle, or it may tickle him a little.

2. If you are worried about gagging when you insert his whole penis into your mouth, moisten your hand and rub the shaft while you are inserting him into your mouth. Keep stroking him the entire time (be sure to lubricate your hand often with saliva), and this way you only have to take him in until your reach your hand. You can train your gag reflex to allow for his cock to travel very far down your throat; this is a mind exercise, which I am sure your partner will be happy to let you practice whenever you want.

3. Cover your teeth with your lips so you don't scratch his cock with your teeth. This is also a learned skill that may take some practice, but be conscious of not rubbing your teeth too hard on his dick. A light scratching of your teeth can be very sensuous, but wait to introduce that until after you are very comfortable with rocking his cock.

4. Lick his cock all over is. It's not just about putting it in your mouth. Licking his shaft up and down and all over will provide him a delicious pleasure. Lick his tip all around, and then lick him all around and up and down.

5. Suck the tip. While sucking him all the way in is exciting, you can provide a different kind of stimulation by just sucking the tip of his cock.

6. Suck! While you are inserting his cock into your mouth, actually suck in, so that you are milking his cock with your mouth. This sensation is very exciting for men. Yes, it is a lot of work for you to rub, suck and pump your head up and down, but it's worth it for him.

7. Don't suck. Change it up a bit and simply move your head up and down while his cock fucks your mouth. Part of giving a good blow

job is keeping it interesting and keeping him guessing what you might do next.

8. Use your hands. While you take him into your mouth, stroke the base of his cock with one hand, while you stroke his balls with your other hand. Moisten your hands with saliva and take him on a magic ride.

9. Stimulate his ass. While you are sucking, you may also grab his ass cheeks and press his pelvis up into your face. You may also moisten a finger and gently rub it on his asshole. If you've never done this to him before, be cautious of his reaction. This is a very erogenous zone for most people, but a lot of people do not venture here. You do not need to penetrate here for it to feel good. Just rubbing it will intensify his experience.

10. Once his cock is nice and moist with your saliva, switch it up a bit and just use your hands to keep stroking his shaft while your mouth licks his ball sack. His balls are very sensitive, and after you've given them a nice licking, take them into your mouth and roll them around. Try to take both into your mouth at the same time ... yes, your mouth will be full, but he will be happy! Take it a little further and lick the space between his asshole and his balls, which is said to be a very erotic zone for a man. You may also choose to "rim" his ass with your tongue, while you stroke his cock up and down.

All that sucking, licking and ball play may make him orgasm quickly, so be careful, especially if you still want to get your piece of the action! If he doesn't cum and you're not done, make sure you tell him you'd like your piece of the pie, too! Men need time after an orgasm before they can become hard enough again to give it to you. Let him use his time wisely by pleasuring you with his mouth and his hands.

Now that you've pleased him, it's time to talk intercourse.

LET'S TALK SEXUAL POSITIONS

Missionary

He's on top, you are on the bottom. This traditional pose allows for a lot of skin contact for you and your partner and is the old standby for a reason: you just fit well together this way!

Riding Your Cowboy

He's on the bottom, you are on the top.

You will have the most control in this position and you will be able to get great clitoral stimulation from the friction, and from the angle that the penis enters you can hit the G-spot more easily. This is also a very visual position for men, and men are visual! Think of how you look while you're riding his cock. He'll be watching you as your breasts move up and down and you close your eyes and moan. Grab your hair and pull it up when you know he is watching you. Suck your fingers and pretend it's his cock. The art of seduction is for you as much as it is for him. When you feel desired and sexy, you will be turned on more easily, and you will be able to take your pleasure further.

Doggy Style

You are on your hands and knees, and he is pumping you from behind. This position allows the man to get really deep inside you with his cock. Depending on the length of your man's cock, this position can be erotically awesome and a little dangerous. If this position gets painful, just tell your partner to ease off a little ("Baby, your cock is just so big and long. Can you ease up a little in this position please?").

Variation: Instead of staying on your hands and knees, lie flat on your tummy. Spread your legs so he can enter you easily, but then close your legs. Try it. It will squeeze his cock really good.

Legs Up, Baby

You lie on your back, he lies on top and your legs are on his shoulders.

Variation: Put both legs on one of his shoulders. Again, this position allows for deeper penetration, and it also tightens the vagina, which squeezes his cock more and provides intense pleasure. Way to do your yoga moves while you have sex ... that's multitasking.

Sitting Down

You are sitting on the side of the bed or a chair, and he's between your legs. Or he's sitting on the bed or chair, and you are sitting on him. Both of these positions allow for deep penetration and closeness of your bodies on the top. You will be able to kiss easily, and he will be able to suckle your boobs. If you are on top, you'll have more control. If he's between your legs, be ready to get pumped, as this position allows for easy access to your goodies!

Up Against the Wall

You are up against the wall, he's holding you up and your legs are wrapped around him. This position is not easy to do! It requires strength on the part of the man to hold you up and still be able to move his cock in and out of you. For you, you will need to be prepared to hang on tight with your legs. The wall helps to provide support for you and will make it easier for your man to hold you up.

Spooning

Both of you are lying on your sides, and he is spooning you from behind and inserting his cock into you from the back. This is an incredibly romantic position, as your bodies will be touching at almost every point. Your man can reach around and fondle your breasts and lovingly kiss your neck and your back. Kissing each other on the lips in this position is much more difficult. Because of the angle of this position, it will be difficult for him to go quickly without falling out of you, so use this position if you want to prolong your sexual encounter. Crossing your legs in this position will help to squeeze your vaginal muscles and provide more intensity for you and your partner.

Make sure you provide feedback and guidance all along the way. When your partner listens to your direction, sex is going to get hotter!

Whether you're already in great shape or not, sex can fulfill your daily physical activity requirement. If you have fun having sex and you switch up positions, your body will be stretched in amazing ways, which is great for your muscles.

Try out a few new positions and see what you like. Remember, you will like different things on different days, so experiment and have fun trying.

69!

Just as these two numbers fit so nicely together on top of each other, you can also fit together well if one of you is flipped over and on top of the other person. This is not an intercourse position, but rather a great way for both of you to get a little oral stimulation. It works best if the man lays down on his back. Then you flip yourself, and put your pussy in his face, while giving you the ability to suck his cock at the same time. This is a very erotic position. Your body's are connected at almost all points, and you are both able to get enjoyment from it. You can also try this position while both of you are lying on your side for a little variety.

Kinky Confessional

Colette Dufour's No Laughing Matter

Our bedroom door is usually ajar, but this sunny Saturday morning it was closed. Dan had closed it when he'd returned from his morning visit to the washroom. Only he had forgotten to lock it.

They say the heart of the family usually resides in the kitchen. In our house, it is in both the kitchen and our bedroom. Four kids, their friends and sometimes even our friends frequent our sanctuary regularly. The king size bed is our family's playpen. Contrary to most bedroom rules, there is a TV and a very popular video player in our room — the only such devices in our house, actually. Food is even allowed here. Ten kids have gathered there watching shows at parties. The bed is in line with the door and the hall's foyer. It is fun to start running out there, gaining momentum to make the leap onto the bed.

But this morning it was only Dan and me snuggled up together under the big blue duvet. We had slept in. No blaring alarm clock had awoken us. The TV was unusually silent. The sun streamed in through the windows. Little specks of dust floated in the air, lit up by the bright sunlight. I was wondering if we breathed in those specks of dust every minute of the day, unseen and unfelt, when I felt the warmth of his hand on my bare breast.

He massaged me. I leaned into him. He cuddled up into the crescent shape of my body. His hot breath was on my neck. It tickled me. I squeezed my shoulder up tight against my chin. I smiled. He ran his hand down the slope of my now slender waist and along my thigh. His fingers traced their way back up to cup my buttock. Oh! I shivered. What could be better than this?

I pressed my bum against his crotch. Our bodies were so companionable. We were meant to be together. I reveled in the comfort of his arms, responding to his caress.

Downstairs, the background sound of pots and pans colliding could be heard. The boys' voices drifted up to me. They were unloading the dishwasher. Their voices were a murmur, muted behind the closed door. I wondered what breakfast fare had been pulled out. I was going to make a comment, when I felt his insistence. Neither of us had spoken yet.

His erection was unmistakable. His penis was hard, pressuring my backside. His intention was obvious. I pressed into his groin with my bare butt. Our skin started to sizzle. I felt myself responding to his caresses. My magic hole was warming up, tingling in response to his tender touch.

He had probably planned this from the moment he'd closed the door ever so quietly, I thought. Saturday morning's bliss lay ahead of the busy day. His wife was his to be taken. No kids in the bed. Oh, boy! He was anticipating sex. But I had a surprise for him up my sleeve.

I suddenly threw back the covers and rolled him onto his back, then straddled him. I flicked my long black hair over my bare shoulders and then reached forward and stroked his stomach. And, oh, I was on him and he was in me, and the bed was rocking.

I almost never did this — ride him naked, that is. Usually we huddled under the covers together and coupled quickly, ready at any moment to be interrupted in coitus. Parental sex. Quick, efficient, effective. But not today, this sexy Saturday morning. A thought flashed through my mind as I squeezed him tightly, a perfect Kegel. I must be ovulating! That was the last thought I had, as I placed my hands on his chest. We were long past seduction at this point. My breasts were flopping wildly.

Then I heard the voice.

We both froze, almost in mid-air.

I turned my head. It was Drew. He was standing quietly at the foot of the bed. He was dressed in his favorite yellow sweatshirt. He simply said, "Do you want pancakes for breakfast?"

I said, "Sure."

He still stood there, staring at us, completely unabashed. I added, "Sex isn't a spectator sport, Drew. Do you mind leaving us? Please close the door tight when you go."

He left, and Dan came. I didn't.

I collapsed on the bed and pulled the covers up over me. Dan laughed.

"Phew! That was close!" he said.

"What part of that was close?" I blurted out. "We got caught in The Act."

"Well, sometimes we don't get to the end of the scene before the curtain falls." He added and snuggled up against me, reveling in The Feeling.

I felt like I had to jump up immediately. Get dressed. Rush downstairs. Make coffee. Act cheerful. Like nothing had happened. I jerked as I thought all these spontaneous thoughts at once, guilt-driven options racing through my head.

He sensed my intention and tightened his hold on me. He wrapped his arms around me, held my tight. Whispered in my ear, "That was great. Kinky, even, eh?"

I relaxed. "Yes, it was."

He had always been a caring, compassionate and discreet lover. I was a widow of a widower when he met me, a single mother with two adopted kids. They were the children of my first husband's marriage. They were ten and eight when I married Dan. Dan is ten years older than me and wanted to have more kids right away. He'd said, "You are a strong woman. I am a strong man. Let's have strong kids together."

I immediately had identical twin boys, so in our first year of marriage, Dan became the father of four children. Ian was now fifteen. The twins were in kindergarten.

When I did show up in the kitchen properly attired and sub-dued, I was confronted by an irate son, Ian. He was standing at the kitchen sink. Drew and Marc were at his elbows, handing him their plates. He took them, and the younger boys bounced away. He turned and confronted us. Dan had his coffee cup in his hand. I was reaching into the cupboard for mine, when Ian blocked me, hands on his hips.

"How could you?" He directed his comment to me.

"How could I what?"

"Drew came downstairs from your bedroom and told me you wanted another baby. That you guys were going to have another baby."

"Why would he say that?"

"Drew said you were upstairs sexing. He came into the kitchen, and that's what he said."

"OH." Dan and I started to giggle.

"It's not funny!" Ian said, following with, "How could you have sex when there are kids in the house?"

I looked at Dan, then at Ian. I wasn't sure how to console Ian, and I didn't want to ruin Dan's mood. I said nothing. I didn't have to say anything. Dan said it all, expounding humorously.

"Ian, there always were kids in the house." At this point, I joined in Dan's mirth. Our eyes locked, and we both burst into laughter. We just couldn't help it. We were caught good.

Ian cut into our merriment, commenting, "Well, OK. The sex is OK, I guess. But it's your attitude that stinks. It's unacceptable. You're not taking this seriously. This isn't a laughing matter."

Exploring Other Territory

A Little Ass Play

Ass play can be very exciting and erotic for men and women. Just rubbing the outside of the asshole with lube can enhance your sexual experience … it feels good! Some love it, some are afraid to try it, and others feel much too "dirty" about it. If you or your partner want to venture here but are worried about hygiene, here's my kinky girl tip. You can buy something called a finger cot from the dollar store, pharmacy or grocery store, which is basically a finger condom. Roll it on your finger, and you and your partner can have all the ass play you like!

If you want to take it further, try inserting a small finger into the anus. When you are starting out, just insert the finger and do not remove it all the way. You may move it back and forth a little if you are able to get it in, but it can feel like you need to go to the bathroom once you remove it fully, so be aware of that! Be sure to use a lot of lubricant, as this area does not produce its own lubricant and is very tight and sensitive; you would not want to damage the tissue here in any way. Having anal sex is a process that may take several years of trying before you are able to perfect it. You must be very relaxed and able to relax the muscles in this area enough to allow for penetration. You must trust your partner and know that he will stop as soon as you need him to. Because of the tightness in this area, starting out with a thin, smooth dildo may be a good start.

SENSES AND SEX

If you want to make love more exciting, daring and erotic, you must delight all of the senses. Touch, smell, taste, feel and hearing are all important, and when you blend them all, you can create an intense experience that is truly out of this world.

The crisp smell of latex can make your pussy burn, if you've associated that smell with lovemaking (condoms?!). Your partner's cum or the smell of your own juices on your fingers can push you and your partner into realms of pleasure that would not exist without the delightful sense of smell. The smell of your partner's cologne or deodorant can totally put you over the top.

Some foods can greatly enhance your experience. An interesting fact about pineapple: It can make your sexual fluids taste great! This is true for both men and women, so if you are planning to swallow your man's load, perhaps you want to feed him some pineapple earlier in the day? My man always winks at me when he eats pineapple.

REMOVING THE SENSES TO HEIGHTEN OTHERS

Being blindfolded causes all of your other remaining senses to become heightened, so use this to your advantage.

Take turns being blindfolded and doing the blindfolding, and then play little games, such as:

- Guess the food item: Gather up some yummy treats to feed your partner. Choose a variety of foods with different consistencies and flavors. Be sure to choose things your partner will enjoy. This is not the time to introduce your partner to new foods! Keep it tasty and fun and comfortable.
- Guess the body part. While your partner is blindfolded, place different parts of your body in his hands, mouth or crotch. Have him guess which part of your body he is sucking, licking or feeling. Reward him when he is right with a kiss, a lick or a touch on his body.

Being blindfolded can be a highly erotic experience, but it may also be a little scary, depending on your comfort level. It does require trust to allow someone else to feed you or touch you or taste you, when you can't see what's going to happen next. The experience of anticipating what will happen next, rather than knowing what's going to happen, is like giving up a little control, but the reward can be highly erotic and exciting.

Experimenting with different temperatures can delight your touch senses. Cold draws of an ice cube over different parts of your body can ignite shivers of pleasure, while warm chocolate sauce can heat up your body parts with a delicious sweetness.

Don't use a spoon or fork to feed your partner. Use your fingers, your boobies and your nipples and then eat food off of your partner's body. Men's nipples can be quite sensitive, and gently licking honey off of his nipples can be an extremely erotic experience for both of you, especially with a blindfold on. Turn his cock into a delicious lollipop by adding some of your favorite sweet sauces to it before playfully eating your dessert.

Have your partner guess the food he is eating or the body part he is licking. Make a game of it, and see where the game takes you. No matter what, you'll both end up winning this game.

While your partner is blindfolded, use different textiles to stimulate his body parts. Here are a few neat things to use:

- Feathers
- Silk
- Cold metal
- Leather
- Satin
- Lace

Use all of the senses to create your sexual masterpiece!

CHAPTER 9

Taking it Further:
Playing Hard

· · · · · · · · · · ·

*"Few things in life seem more
sexy than a banned book."*
— Chuck Palahniuk

There is a fine line between pleasure and pain, and at the heights of pleasure, a little pain can take your orgasm to the moon! A little pinch of a nipple, or a slap on the ass at just the right time may be just the things you need to launch you upward!

If you've never experienced the pleasure of a playful slap on the ass, it's time you gave it a slap! Slapping your own ass is exciting, especially if you want to make someone else watching you HOT! Otherwise, it's really great to have your ass slapped by someone else.

Most of us will associate being spanked with being in trouble; it's a punishment often given out by a parent. Good Lord, what could be kinky about that?

Well, playful slaps from your partner can enhance your pleasure, if you're into it. In order for sexual slapping to be sexy and pleasurable, you've got to follow some rules.

You or your partner must want to be spanked. So, you may need to ask for it ("Slap my ass, baby!") or ask if you can do it to him. Once you have established yourselves in a relationship, you will get to know what your partner wants. BUT, pay attention to your partner. He may not always want something he's liked in the past. Watch his body language and ask questions like, "You like that, baby? You want me to do it again?"

Be willing to voice your opinion and provide guidance to your partner: "Baby, that's enough slapping for tonight, please" or "Slap me harder, baby!"

If you enjoy spanking or being spanked, try using a whip to take this pleasure further. There are different styles of whips, and some hurt more than others. Start off small and work your way up if you're into it. It can be very empowering to lovingly whip someone's ass or have your own whipped. It's playful and it allows you to explore your trust relationship.

Always stop when you need to stop and always respect your partner's desire to stop. Be honest! Just because your partner likes doing it doesn't mean you have to like it or that you will like it right now.

Never allow it to get to a point where you start resenting your partner for not seeing the signs that you're done. Take responsibility for yourself and be kinky enough to give direction and correction.

What are you willing to try that you've never tried before?

Explore your sexuality and your threshold for creating pleasure. Sex is not meant to be painful; it is always meant to be a source of pleasure and release.

I could never be kinky enough for my husband, but that's OK! He pushes me further than I would take myself in the bedroom, and I trust him. He always knows when I've reached my limit.

Have a safe word no matter what you venture into. It may mean stop, it may mean let's get the heck out of here or it may mean slow it down. Decide on a word or words that will allow you a little control over a situation where you will not be in control!

If you're comfortable, try out something new and see how it feels. Try it more than once before you make a solid judgment — it may depend on your mood and on your partner. You are learning something new, so there will always be a learning curve.

Learn About Toys

There are home parties you can have that focus on pleasure toys. Attending or hosting one of these parties in the comfort of your own home or a friend's home can be a comfortable way of exploring the exciting world of sex toys in a very non-threatening way. You will get to see all kinds of different vibrators, G-spot tools, lubricants and other gadgets you can fill your bedroom toolbox with. Whether you are new to bedroom toys or an old pro, these parties can be a great way to learn different techniques, as well as keep up on all the newest sex gadgets. It's really quite amazing to see the selection of toys that are available. Some look just like the real thing; others are bright colors and are shaped liked different animals ... beavers, dolphins or totem poles. Some vibrate, some don't. Some have clitoral stimulation, and some don't. Some have 10 settings and twist, vibrate and rock your clit. Some have pearls that move up and down the shaft while it is inside you, and some have remote controls so your partner can take the lead on your stimulation.

If you've never had a toy before, a home party is a great way to be able to feel all of the toys in a comfortable setting. You won't know what you like until you try them. Remember, toys are not just for your use. Toys can really enhance your experience together in the bedroom. Your partner will have much more control over what he does to you if he's using a dildo ... and if it has lots of different settings, he can take you up and down the mountain of pleasure over and over again.

The Toy Chest

It's exciting to add toys to your bedroom play. Here are a few cool things you can consider adding to your collection.

- Dildo: These simulated penises come in all shapes and sizes and colors, moving or not moving, with clitoral stimulation or not. Budget is a factor here. The more real a dildo feels and looks and the more functions it has, generally the higher the price.
- Nipple clamps: There are a wide variety of these also. Some just clip on to provide a consistent pinch to your nipples, some have a chain in between the clamps, so your partner can pull on them and some are adjustable so you can change the pressure of the pinch on the nipple.
- Clitoral stimulators: These come in a wide variety of shapes and sizes. Some are dolphin-shaped and vibrating, while others have bumps on them and do not vibrate. Explore the world of clitoral toys, and you will be surprised and excited by all of the possibilities! There is even one you can wear, and it has a remote control. Your partner could have the remote and use it to make you orgasm while you are at dinner or a movie. Or you could use it yourself while you are in the middle of a boring meeting at work. Just think of the possibilities!
- Tickle toys: Being tickled in a sexual way is very stimulating to the skin, and it can make you writhe with pleasure and beg for more. Being touched softly with a feather or a silk scarf run lightly down your body feels incredible. Do it blindfolded and you can really enhance the touch sensations over your whole body.
- G-spot toy: This looks like a little curved spoon, and it is designed to hit your G-spot. If you're still searching for this spot, the tool can

be an exciting way to find it yourself or an incredible way to have your partner go on an adventure mission.

- Anal beads: These little balls are all connected along a long strip, with the beads increasing in size as you move along the strip. Insert the beads into your anus (using lots of lubrication), starting with the smallest bead first and going in as far as you want to go. Leave them in while you stimulate your other areas, either on your own or with a partner. When you are reaching the height of your orgasm, grab your beads yourself or have your partner grab them and pull the strip out quickly. The sensation will make your orgasm even more intense.

- Ben Wa balls: These balls are inserted into the vagina, and you must squeeze your kegel muscles around them to keep them in. They are very good for strengthening your kegel muscles so you can have more control over squeezing your man's cock in the right way during intercourse.

Note: Just because you're kinky doesn't mean you are promiscuous! Men are drawn to sexual charm, so be aware that the more sexiness you put out, the more attention you will get.

BONDAGE

Getting All Tied Up

Having intense pleasure requires you to give your body and your mind over to someone you trust so that you can experience sexual joy. Being tied up relinquishes your control and gives the power to your partner. Giving yourself over completely can be hard to do. At least you still have your mouth to provide guidance — that is, until your partner gags you. Just kidding. Unless you're into that kind of thing!

The appeal of tying is in the surrendering to your partner. It's like saying, "I give myself over to you to do as you please, so please me often."

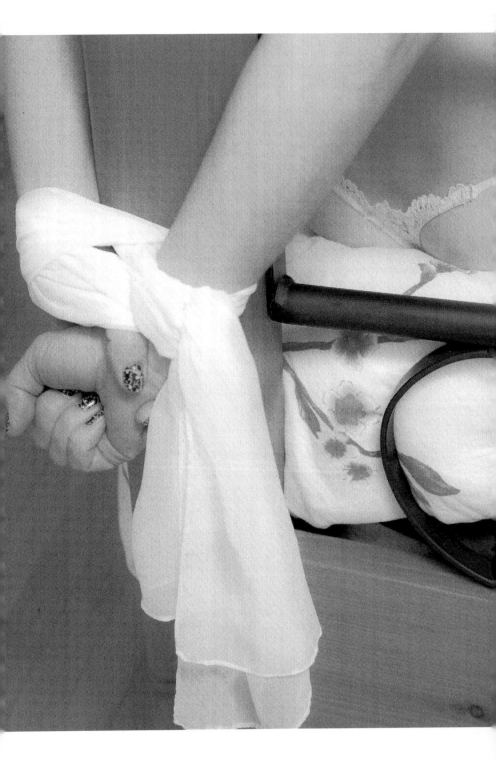

If you've never tried being tied, try it. And then tie your partner up and have your way with him. Intensify your pleasure and give yourselves to each other.

KINKY CONFESSIONAL

Dawn's Change of Scenery

It was my birthday, and my husband and I had a date night planned. We arranged for a babysitter for our children and headed out for supper. He had planned this entire night for me, starting with reservations at a new restaurant. The dinner was spectacular, and the company was sweet. With no kids, the attention could be just on us. After dinner, we started our drive home, and my husband made what I thought was a wrong turn.

"Babe, where are you going?" I asked.

He replied, "Oh, I just thought we'd make a little detour on the way home." A little stream of pleasure and excitement started, and I was intrigued by his "detour." I love surprises. He parked the car and said, "Come on, let's walk our dinner off." We got out of the car, and I watched as my husband pulled a full backpack out of the trunk and slung it on his back. He smiled slyly at me and said, "Come on, babe."

We walked down the block of a residential street and then up a set of wooden stairs surrounded by trees. In my head, I thought, *Where the heck is he taking me?*

At the top of the stairs, my husband led me to a very well manicured stretch of grass, which just happened to be the ninth hole of a golf course!

Shocked and a little afraid of trespassing, I gave my husband the *"What are you thinking?"* look. He smiled and starting unpacking his backpack. The first item out was a blanket, which he spread on the green and had me sit on. He sat down beside me and gave me a frisky embrace and then unpacked the rest of his bag.

It was a midnight picnic: a bottle of wine, a corkscrew, chocolate, fruit and two glasses. We were under the stars; the moon shone brightly, and any chill in the air was replaced by the heat we were throwing off! I was totally impressed with his planning! His moonlight picnic was delightful. We sipped wine under the stars, we fed each other fruit and chocolate, we talked and we sipped more wine. We chatted intimately and giggled over the sheer craziness of what we were doing. With the wine, the setting and the romance, it wasn't long before we were passionately kissing and frantically trying to get into each other's pants! Soon we were naked and we made love by the light of the moon on that smooth, manicured green. As we lay spent and dreamy eyed, I thought of two things. One: Why did I not have Kleenex in my purse? I was a little wet down there. And two: How lucky I was to have a partner who was willing to seduce me after all of our years of marriage, to put the effort into surprising and delighting us both with a little change of scenery.

COUPLES' CLUBS

Couples' clubs or sex clubs are in every city. If you want to be sexy around other people in a safe and comfortable place, a sex club is a great place to dress to your sexy nines and release your inhibitions. Sex clubs aren't cheap, and some allow couples only. This is not a meat market or a place where singles go to find a partner. These clubs are designed for people to explore their sexuality to a deeper level. Some clubs have hot tubs and pools, couches and beds. Decide what you want to get out of your club experience and discuss it with your partner before you venture out. Look at the clubs in your area online and see which one seems more appealing to your taste. The clubs will list their rules and etiquette on their sites so you have some idea of what to expect. Some clubs have dress codes (small white towel only), and others just encourage sexy dress. Some have theme nights for taking dressing up to the next level, and most serve alcohol.

Always discuss the rules of the game with your partner before you hit the club. What are you willing to do, or not do? How far are you willing to go? Communicate with each other about what the goals of the night are before you go so you can both keep each other in check, and so no one ends up getting hurt as far as emotions go. You may choose to change your ideals once you are there, but it's best that you both know where each of you are starting when it comes to the expectations.

Ready to take what you've learned out into the field?

CHAPTER 10

Practice What You've Learned with Five Steamy Nights of Kink

"Sex appeal is fifty percent what you've got and fifty percent what people think you've got."
— Sophia Loren

KINKY NIGHT #1

Burlesque Your Partner!

Burlesque is a theatrical display to entice your partner. It's not just what you show, it's how you show it. Slow and sexy, playful and fun — use this as a way to slow things down, change up the rhythm and create deep desire.

This requires confidence in yourself, which we have been working on. You are sexy, and your partner deserves a show!

You don't have to choreograph anything, and he doesn't have to know what you have planned.

All you need is a chair you can straddle, a pretty bra and panties, a sexy outfit and a great pair of sexy shoes or boots. You may choose to wear a sexy outfit that takes time to take off (lots of buttons on your shirt, etc.). You can also use accessories, like a feather boa, hat or glasses. Feel free to "dress the part" of the seductress.

Tell your partner that you have something special for him. Have your partner sit on the bed (or couch). Place your chair in front of him, but not too close to him. Turn on some steamy, passionate music. (Have a few songs picked out that suit your taste.)

Rules for this exercise? Your partner stays fully clothed the whole time. You can touch your partner, but he is not allowed to touch you! (Until you decide to change those rules!) If your partner just can't keep his hands off you while you are performing, have a scarf on hand to playfully tie his hands behind his back! He won't know what hit him when you decide to become a tantalizing burlesque stripper … but he's going to love it! Start your music and begin your routine. Here are few ideas to try out.

Straddle the chair. Wink at your partner and blow him kisses.

Turn the chair around so you are straddling it and your back is to your partner. Hold the back of the chair and bend backwards so your hair hangs down and your partner gets a glimpse of your cleavage.

Gyrate (rock your hips back and forth and around) while you are on the chair.

Stand up and to the side of the chair. Stick your ass out and bend forward.

Look desirously at your partner and erotically suck on one of your fingers. Little teasing licks and long deep sucks that take your finger(s) all the way into your mouth. Imagine what you are making him think about!

Dance around the chair, showing off your assets.

Have your back to your partner and slap your ass, then look over your shoulder sneakily at your partner and slap your ass again!

Start slowly undoing buttons on your clothes. The more slowly you can remove your clothes, the better. You don't want to reveal too much too quick.

Standing to the side of the chair, put one leg up on the chair and show him your panty-covered pussy. Using the palm of your hand, gently slap your pussy a few times while you stare intently into your partner's eyes. Look playfully down at your pussy and slowly slide your panties to the side to reveal your pink wetness. Look at your partner and wink … then put the panties back! Little peeks at nipples and boobies will keep the desire building!

Touch yourself as much as you can while you are burlesquing your partner. Run your hand slowly and sensually down your arm or your leg. Caress yourself as you would want someone to caress you. He will be wishing it was his hands all over you … and that's the point!

No matter what you take off, leave your pretty bra and panties (or other lingerie) on, as well as your shoes, until you decide you are ready. Wearing high heels may make it more awkward to dance around, so don't feel like you have to boogie heavily or quickly. Use your body to make sexual movements. High heels are extremely sexy, and men (and women) love garter belts with nylons. Extreme sexiness!

Move closer to your partner as the songs play. Squeeze your breasts together and put his face in your cleavage. Don't leave it there long! Just a little feel is all he needs.

Sit down on his lap. By now, you should be able to feel his excitement. Grind yourself on your partner's lap and give him the lap dance of his life. Sit with your back to him and lean forward while you grind. Then flip around and straddle him face to face. Rub your hands in his hair and gently grab and pull it a little; you are in control. If you have a feather boa or a scarf of any kind, drape it around his neck and shoulders and use it to pull him closer to you, into your cleavage. The feathers have an incredible soft, sensual feeling, as do silk scarves. Use the power of touch to invoke passion!

You may choose to practice a few moves before you blatantly seduce your man, but don't worry if you don't! Your body will know what to do when you get into the music and when you are in the mood.

It's okay if you feel the need to spontaneously giggle while you are doing this, especially if you are new to it. Dancing sexy can feel awkward, and you may feel nervous about how you look doing it! REMEMBER: Your partner is so extremely excited right now by ANYTHING you do that it won't matter at all. Laugh it out and then get back into character!

Here are some great songs for this exercise:

- "You Can Leave Your Hat On" – Joe Cocker (Coincidence that he has "cock" in his name?)
- "Pour Some Sugar on Me" – Def Leppard
- "Glory Box" – Portishead
- "Sexual Healing" – Marvin Gaye
- "Feel Like Making Love" – Roberta Flack
- "Fever" – Peggy Lee
- "Diamonds Are a Girl's Best Friend" – Marilyn Monroe
- "Lady Marmalade" – Patti LaBelle original (See the video by Christina Aguilera, Lil' Kim, Mya and Pink for some burlesque-y ideas!)

Make yourself a little playlist. Start off with something slow, then increase the tempo, and then slow it down again! Have fun with this!

Let passion and desire take its course, and when you can't take the pressure anymore, let your partner touch you and let the rest be blissful history!

Let your partner know that the next time, it's his turn to burlesque YOU! There is nothing sexier than having your partner seduce you. Let your partner read the above section, and then turn the tables the next time you have a date night at home. It will be his turn to tie your hands behind your back and playfully seduce you with a clever strip tease. Remind him to take his socks off; a half-naked man with his socks still on can take the heat out of any strip tease!

Being "burlesqued," as opposed to doing the "burlesquing," is a very different experience. Sharing the lead on this exciting game of passion will ensure that both you and your partner have a chance to experience the excitement of both positions. It's a little powerful to be the one teasing, yet it's also very thrilling to be the one getting tantalizingly played with.

KINKY NIGHT #2

The Lingerie Shop

This kinky outing begins at the mall. Meet your partner at your favorite mall and tell him you need his help picking out a couple of items. You can either surprise him or tell him what you're in the market for. Head to the lingerie store and leisurely browse the sexy selections.

This can be an incredibly eye-opening experience for you. Find out which styles your partner likes, and which colors. Leather or lace, innocent and soft or rough and dirty. You will have your own tastes, so choose items to try on that appeal to you. As long as you feel sexy, your partner should respond appropriately.

Your partner may have widely varied taste in lingerie compared to you. Don't judge! If they show you something they like, make a mental note and nod. Remember, this is meant to be a learning experience as much as it is a turn-on date night. Get to know your partner's taste and cater to it.

If he likes leather, give him leather! If he likes lace, give him that, too. If he just loves it all, have fun collecting and sharing your sexy outfits with him.

If he goes gaga over garter belts and stockings and you are not really sure, just try it for him one time. It's like the one bite rule:

see how it tastes first (and maybe one more time). You never know if you'll like it unless you try it. If it's been a while since you tried it, try it again. Your tastes change all the time.

You should expect your partner to cater to your every desire also. When you please others, you will feel happy, and they will be very pleased.

KINKY NIGHT #3

Blind Dessert

Before you begin, prepare small bowls of bite-sized treats to tempt your partner with. Do not let him see what you are preparing. You want him to have a chance to guess the food you are going to feed him. The thrill of not knowing what he's being fed will add intensity to this exercise. Have your partner sitting up in your bed or on the couch. Blindfold him and make it good — you don't want him to see at all! Dim the lights and make it romantic. Turn on some soft, romantic music and get the food items you have prepared. Chat like you would on any other regular night and then tell your partner that you are going to feed him his dessert. (Well, the pre-dessert, because the icing on this cake will be coming soon!)

Here are some great options for treats for this hot night:

- Chocolate
- Chocolate covered strawberries
- Chocolate sauce (you can see where my mind is...chocolate!)
- Whip cream
- Honey
- Caramel sauce
- Olives
- Cheese
- Oysters

- Assorted fruits: grapes, strawberries, blueberries, raspberries, pineapple (be sure to cut into bite-sized pieces)
- Ice cream
- Ice
- Deli/Italian meats
- Bite-sized morsels of his favorite desserts (brownies, cookies, cake)
- Pudding, crème caramel
- Chips and dip

Kinky Night #4

Strip Club

Strip clubs are not just for men and can be very exciting when you go with your partner! If you've never gone to see the strippers, it's time to check out what all the fuss is about. Sure, you'll go broke buying a drink or two there, but usually women don't have to pay the standard cover charge and the experience will be well worth it. If there was more demand for male strip clubs, I'd say take your partner there, but us women don't feel the need to pay for this type of things, so male strip joints are few and far between. Ain't nothin' sexier than a hot, sexy man who can dance while taking his clothes off just for you. If you can find one and convince your partner to go with you, head to the male strippers!

Your partner, however, may not feel the same way about watching another man strip, but if you'll do it for him, he should be prepared to go the distance for you.

On this night out, you will likely be off to watch beautiful women take their clothes off for both of you.

Watching female strippers together can be a total turn-on. Just walking into a club on the arm of your knight in shining armor is sure to turn a few heads. Wear something sexy and kinky, like a skirt with no panties, some sexy heels and a low-cut, cleavage-showing top. Make him proud of the sexy goddess he's got on his arm.

Buy a few expensive drinks and delight in the shows you are about to watch. Appreciate the beauty of each girl who hits the floor. Appreciate how much effort the ladies put into their bodies, their costumes and their dance moves. See how they use their moves to create desire in their customers. Use this night as research. Get costume ideas and dance moves that you can try out when you get home. After your expensive drinks are done and your panties are wet, it's time to go home and make all of his dreams come true.

KINKY NIGHT #5

Sex Shops or Shows

There are a variety of specialty sex stores in every city. Going to one with your partner can make for a fulfilling dessert after a lovely dinner date! There are many types of sex stores. Some are high-end and fairly classy, and others may be a little seedy. Choose one that appeals to you and your partner and make a date out of it.

Take time to wander the aisles together and see what kind of things are on the shelves. Ask questions without embarrassment. The staff work in a sex store, for goodness sake. It's their job to know about the products and how to use them for maximum effect. It is only you that will be embarrassed, so just get rid of that feeling and call it excitement instead. You will be able to check out personal lubricants, lingerie, porn mags and videos, costumes and a variety of toys and tools. Choose an item together and go home and try it out. It will make your panties wet just walking the aisles, and the anticipation of using your new purchase will have you on the edge of orgasm before you even walk through the bedroom door.

Most major cities will have a sex show at least once per year. These events are normally on the weekend, and it is like a trade-show for the sex industry, so it's a great chance to see what's out there and get your kinky on together. Get tickets for you and your partner and make a date out of it! Dress up a little sexy and have fun with this. Be prepared to see anything and everything to do with sex at these shows: advanced bondage straps, sex swings, whips, chains, leather, lace, costumes, toys and porn. This is the place to see it all and not feel bad about exploring and learning together. Ask as many questions as you can, read brochures and have fun!

There is always entertainment at these shows, so you'll likely get to see a strip show or two (men and women). The local firemen usually have a booth, so you can get your signed calendar and meet a few of the hotties themselves. You will be amazed at the selection of items available for purchase, and you will be surprised at the number of people who attend these shows. And it's "normal" people who go, just like you and me. Everyone has a little kink in them, but no one has to know about it!

This is a great opportunity to show each other the kinds of things you like. You can learn a lot about your partner, and he can learn a lot about your tastes in sex. Is he ready to learn more? Have him read on and take some pointers from me about how to please you.

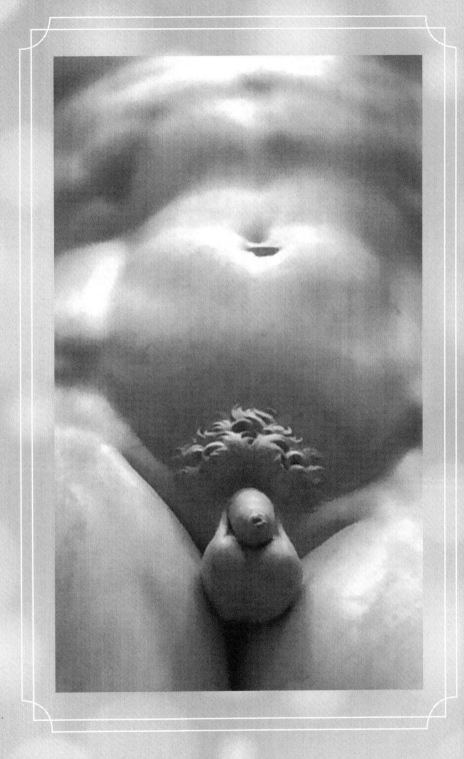

CHAPTER 11

For His Eyes Only

· ·

*"The noblest pleasure
is the joy of understanding."*
– Leonardo da Vinci

MANSCAPING! CLEAR THE JUNGLE, TARZAN!

I know you like your kinky girl to be smooth and soft as silk. Hair-free, smelling good, dressed sexily and trimmed just the way you like it. Your girl spends a lot of time nourishing and treating her body right, with love, attention and focus.

Ensure that you are doing the same with your body! When you take care of your body, you tell the world that you feel like you are worth it and that you know you deserve to be treated with respect and love. Appearances do matter, and your girl will respond positively to you if you make sure you are adding effort to the treatment of your body.

BECOME LIKE ADONIS, GREEK GOD OF BEAUTY AND DESIRE

Be sure to tame the beast below. You don't have to go hair-free like the Egyptians did (unless you want to), but you should spend a little time making sure your pubes are staying tidy and neat at the base of your cock. A little trim can go a long way. Trimming back some of the hair at the base can make your cock look even larger than it already is, and there will be less chance of your girl getting a mouthful of hair when she's got you thoroughly inserted.

I know that blow jobs are king and that there can never be enough of them, so you need to make your junk as appealing as you can.

Shower regularly and, to quote the Beastie Boys, "If you wash your ass, you'd best use soap!"

Be sure you are clean and that you smell great. When you put attention into caring for your body, it shows. You will attract more goodness to your body when it is treated sweetly.

Take care of your teeth, and have fresh breath. Trim your fingernails and your toenails and keep them clean. Your goddess deserves to be touched with clean, smooth hands and nails.

Wear sexy underwear, instead of your favorite ripped and holey ones. Underwear does matter! Ask your partner what style of underwear she likes. Remember, she wears uncomfortable, sexy lingerie for you, so pony up and wear what she wants.

She is going to want to share her deepest fantasies and desires with you. Do your best to make her dreams come true. If she dreams of firemen, give her a night of dress up and fire rescue in your own bedroom. If she wants you to strip for her, do it.

Your goal is to please each other, and that can take effort.

Women take longer to get in the mood. They need at least 20 minutes to be solidly under your love spell. Take the time to get her in the mood. It may take 20 minutes, but just bending her over and expecting her to take your cock in the first few minutes is a little unreasonable. Get her into it first.

If she's feeling stressed and overwhelmed by the amount of tasks she has to complete, ask if you can help. Or just take care of some things for her on your own. Reducing the amount of things racing in her head can give you a solid pathway to her passion. Her knight in shining armor would do anything, including dishes, laundry, bathrooms or cooking, to please his queen. Show her that you mean business.

Rub her back, her legs, her arms. Treat her to a 10-minute massage and use oil to enhance her experience. While you massage, be careful not to touch her in her erogenous zones (boobies, pussy or ass). Just being sensually touched by you for 10 minutes will be getting her in the mood, and she will be thinking about you touching her, so let her build up a little before you give her what she wants.

Play sexy music, light candles, set up the bedroom like a sexy grotto. Add effort into your sexual routine. Make her know that you care about her and your sex life and that you are willing to do almost anything to please her.

Dance with your partner in the bedroom. Get the sexy music going, and say, "May I have this dance, my lady?"

Snuggle in close together and just hug and move your bodies. You don't have to know how to dance with your partner. Just stand together and sway to the beat of the music. Touch each other. Hold her like you'll never let her go.

Surprise her with flowers, chocolates, jewelry, lingerie or sex toys. We all love surprises, and the fact that you thought about them and then shopped for them, may make them more receptive to your advances. It will put you in their good books, for sure! If you are going to buy lingerie, buy her something you would like to see her in, regardless of her tastes. Tell he you think she would look fiery hot in that outfit and that you cannot wait to see it on her.

Plan date nights, where spending quality time together is more important than the sex. (Even though the sex may be the goal.)

Making dinner reservations, packing picnic lunches or taking her somewhere exciting will get you far.

Run her a bath and then join her after a while, or just offer to wash her hair for her. She will love having you wash her hair and her body with your strong, willing hands. Show her how sensitive you can be with her body, and her mind will be yours to hold.

Adding romance to your already excellent regime will not only please her, it will please you, too! You will start enjoying preparing all the "little things" and you will be thinking more about your partner and pleasure than the other distractions in your life.

Make it known that you worship her body. Tell her how beautiful, sexy and amazing she is. Notice and appreciate her clothing, her hair, her nails and her shoes, even if you've lost count of them. Compliment her and let her know you are thinking about her.

You can romance her all night, and it will never get old.

Give her space, time and compassion. Talk dirty to her and talk sweetly to her. Make her feel like she is your queen and that you will feed her grapes and pour her wine for as long as she would like. Build her up. Tease her with your tantalizing touch and your sultry smooth voice. Tell her what you are going to do to her. Make her beg for you to do more!

Have fun with this! Making a woman happy is challenging but not impossible.

Beware that what works once may not work the same again. Be receptive to her body language, and if something's not working, try something else. Ask her what she wants. Ask her if she is enjoying what you are doing. Ask her permission to take it further.

Communicate your desires and listen to hers. If it's been a while since you hopped in the sack to do more than sleep, don't use it as a negative against either of you. Simply move forward and try something new.

Do a little online research on different ways to please a woman. Watch a few videos, get a few new ideas and then surprise your partner with them. Watch her reaction when you pull out a new lick or sucking action. Keep what works and modify to suit you both. Don't be afraid to try new things. They're not all going to work, but something will, and you'll both be rewarded!

Just by putting your energy into sex and pleasure, you will heighten your bond and ensure that more of your nights are steamy instead of dreamy!

She picked up this book because she wants to get more good loving. Use that to your advantage!

Make it fun, sexy, surprising and delicious, and you'll be rewarded.

CONCLUSION

Being that Kinky Girl is all about you being comfortable with yourself and being comfortable sharing your beautiful self with yourself and others. I want you to take pleasure from your life as a woman and enjoy all that life has to offer you. I want you to release your inhibitions and stretch yourself further than you have gone before. I want you to want your man. I want you to want yourself. I want you to love your body and feel excited about the pleasure that touching and being touched can bring you. You are perfect just as you are now, and you are worth every minute of pleasure you get in your life.

No matter what you do with your costumes, candles or lingerie, the whole point of all of this is that you (and hopefully your partner) are thinking about your sex life. You are making it a priority. You are adding intention and positive, steamy energy. You are trying new things, talking to your partner and allowing yourself time to have a wonderful sex life.

You are making your sex life important to you, and when you do that, you will be excited about all that effort. You will be chasing your passion, and your results are going to astound you. Having more fun in the bedroom is your decision to make for yourself.

You are here to have fun. Enjoy the adventure, Have a lot of sex — great sex. Get kinky, and then get kinkier.

Yours in Kinkiness,
Tina

ACKNOWLEDGEMENTS

Book number 3 in the Be That Series is now complete! What started as a tiny seed of a thought has now grown into a series of books that have changed my life and the lives of many of my fans. I want to take this opportunity to thank all of the people who have helped and inspired me to get to this amazing book.

Firstly, to my mom, who has always been there for me, inspired me and been the kinkiest lady in my life! Mom, you are an inspiration to so many people, but you have always inspired me to just be me. You have watched our children while Ryan and I took much needed breaks away from our children to reconnect and keep the steam going in our lives.

To my stepfather Don, you have always supported my mom through everything and you make her so happy. You and my mom are an inspiration to couples everywhere, and I love how much you love each other and how kinky you are together! No matter what age you are, you can be kinky and have fun with each other!

To my Father, Ken. As a successful businessman, you have inspired me to always be my best, and never be satisfied working for someone else. This entrepreneurial spirit keeps the fire inside me going and it lights me up when I get down. Your support and success is amazing, and I want you to know that I appreciate everything you have done for me.

To my sister, Brenda, who blushes when my mom and I talk "sex," this one's for you, my sweet baby sister. I hope you are red in the face the whole time you read this book. Here's to many more Wednesdays!

To my very best friends, Annie and James, thank you for allowing me to write this book while we cruised the Mediterranean together. You have always been the most supportive, amazing friends a couple could have, and I am looking forward to spending another 50 years as best friends, raising our kids, traveling, and playing cards together. Annie, thank you for your advice and continued support with my books. You are the most avid reader I know and one of the smartest women I have ever met.

To my niece Brooke, you have always been there for me, and I will always be here for you. Thanks for making sure I get to places on time, and that I look good when I get there! You have donated hours of your time to chauferring and primping me for tv, as well as babysitting your sweet little cousins. You will always have a special place in my heart reserved just for you.

To my photographer, Wendell, I know that it was not a coincidence that we met. You and I see eye to eye, and it made the photo shoot for this book go so smoothly. Thanks for all the planning on this one, and I am looking forward to the next one!

To my designer, Tania Craan. You are always amazing, you keep me on track and your ideas are always brilliant. Your advice, patience and promptness are appreciated, and I am looking forward to working on more books with you!

To my cousin Julie, who has dedicated her time to me, through thick and thin. Julie, thank you for your support, your love and your generosity. You inspire me every day to be a better person, and whether you're buying a homeless man a pop or being a surrogate for a couple in need, you bring sunshine to people's lives in ways that others never even think about.

To Amy, who was the inspiration behind this book.

To all my fans, and authors who contributed works and stories to this book, I thank you for opening up to me and sharing your stories with the world. You are the reason I keep writing.

Love and Sunshine to all of you…Tina.

Coming up next….Be That Millionaire.

www.bethatbooks.com

Be That Kinky Girl

Proudly Published by

Be Inspired.
Be Motivated.
Be Entertained.

www.bethatbooks.com

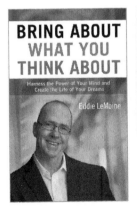

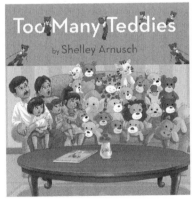

Made in the USA
Charleston, SC
17 November 2014